Pearson Scott Foresman

Writing Rubrics and Anchor Papers

Glenview, Illinois
Boston, Massachusetts
Chandler, Arizona
Upper Saddle River, New Jersey

ISBN-13: 978-0-328-47652-7
ISBN-10:   0-328-47652-8

8 9 10 V031 15 14 13 12

Contents

Writing Models

Weekly Rubrics

Support for Writing

Suggestions for Using This Book

This book is most effective when used in conjunction with the weekly writing lessons and unit writing process lessons in Scott Foresman's *Reading Street.* Rubrics and anchor papers can be copied and distributed or made into transparencies. Here are some ways to use the materials.

- Distribute copies of page v to students. Work through the explanations of traits with the class to develop background for discussing scores.

- Display one-by-one the four models for a given mode in order (starting with Score 1 or Score 4). Work through the commentaries that appear along with the models to illustrate how each got its score.

- After students become proficient with determining scores, distribute copies of writing models from this book with the scores screened out. Work with students to arrive at scores.

- Display a model that is Score 1. Work with students to improve the model.

- Display the rubric for the type of writing you are teaching. Have students use the rubric to evaluate their own writing.

- Distribute copies of the Self-Evaluation Guide on page vi. Have students use this guide to evaluate their work.

Tips for Teaching and Evaluating Writing

- Choose one writing trait to emphasize each week. Appoint a team of students for each trait. Have them find their trait in selections they read and in their own writing and present their findings to the class.

- Read short passages from literature (for example, a tall tale) and from other content areas (for example, a science text). Point out how writer's purpose determines voice, word choice, and style.

- Remember that a writer may be more proficient in one trait than in another. To arrive at a score, evaluators must weigh proficiency in all traits.

- Tell students that when they evaluate their own writing, assigning a score of 3, 2, or even 1 does not necessarily indicate a failure. The ability to identify areas for improvement in future writing is a valuable skill.

- Encourage students to think of themselves as writers. Alert them that subjects, words, and ideas are everywhere. Suggest they keep a notebook handy to record material, such as overheard conversations, sentences from their reading, and vivid words they encounter.

- Join students as they write. Share your own writing with them and ask for their feedback on your work.

- Model constructive ways of giving feedback on writing. *(Words such as* pounce *and* swat *give me a good picture of your cat. You said her name is Boots. How did she get that name? You mentioned that she has a favorite place to sleep. Could you describe it?)*

Traits

- Focus/Ideas
- Organization
- Voice
- Word Choice
- Sentences
- Conventions

- **Focus/Ideas** refers to the main purpose for writing and the details that make the subject clear and interesting. It includes development of ideas through support and elaboration.

- **Organization** refers to the overall structure that guides readers through a piece of writing. Within that structure, transitions show how ideas, sentences, and paragraphs are connected.

- **Voice** shows the writer's unique personality and establishes a connection between writer and reader. Voice, which contributes to style, should be suited to the audience and the purpose for writing.

- **Word Choice** is the use of precise, vivid words to communicate effectively and naturally. It helps create style through the use of specific nouns, lively verbs and adjectives, and accurate, well-placed modifiers.

- **Sentences** covers strong, well-built sentences that vary in length and type. Skillfully written sentences have pleasing rhythms and flow fluently.

- **Conventions** refers to mechanical correctness and includes grammar, usage, spelling, punctuation, capitalization, and paragraphing.

Self-Evaluation Guide

Name ____

Name of Writing Product _______________________________________

Directions Review your final draft. Then rate yourself on a scale from 4 to 1 (4 is a top score) on each writing trait. After you fill out the chart, answer the questions.

Writing Traits	4	3	2	1
Focus/Ideas				
Organization				
Voice				
Word Choice				
Sentences				
Conventions				

1. What is the best part of this piece of writing? Why do you think so?

____

____

____

____

2. Write one thing you would change about this piece of writing if you had the chance to write it again.

____

____

____

____

Writing Models

Write about something funny that happened to you and a pet or another animal.

Rubric	4	3	2	1
Focus/Ideas	Reader can understand the story	Reader can understand part of the story	Reader cannot understand the story very well	Reader cannot understand the story
Organization	Has a good beginning, middle, and end	Has a beginning, middle, and end	Events are out of order	Does not have a beginning, middle, and end
Voice	Clearly shows how the writer feels	Shows a little about how the writer feels	Does not show very well how the writer feels	Does not show the writer feels
Word Choice	Has words that help reader "see" the story	Some words help reader "see" part of the story	Words do not help reader "see" the story	Words are hard to read
Sentences	Sentences not all alike	Sentences are complete	Sentences are not complete	Sentences not complete or clear
Conventions	Uses good spelling and capitalization	Uses fair spelling and capitalization	Uses poor spelling and capitalization	Uses very poor spelling and capitalization

Where Is Trevor?

My dog Trevor is scared of storms. When he hears thunder and lightning, he hides under my bed.

Last week a huge truck dumped a load of dirt at the house across the street. It was noisy. Later, I looked for Trevor. I could not find him. I thought he had run away. Where did I find Trevor? He was under my bed! Maybe he thought the noise was thunder. I was sure happy I found him.

Score 4

Story sticks to the topic and includes specific details. It has a beginning, middle, and end. Writer is involved with the subject. Strong words (*scared, thunder, lightning, dumped, noisy*) create vivid pictures. A question and an exclamation add variety to sentences. Writer uses good grammar, capitalization, and spelling.

Sandy

One day me and my dog Sandy were playing in the snow. She is a Siberian husky and she loves snow. I went outside and I got a snowball. I threw it to Sandy. She jumt up and ate the snowball, and then she jumt on me. Her paws were on my sholders. Then I ran, and she ran after me, and takld me. It was funny. She made me laf hard. That was a fun day.

Score 3

This is a good response to the prompt. The narrative has a clear beginning, middle, and end, and tells how the writer feels about the event described. Sentences are varied, but many begin with *she.* One pronoun error *(me and my dog Sandy were)*, and a few errors in spelling *(jumt, sholders, takld)* do not seriously detract from the writing.

> One day a long time ago I was 4 yers old. I was standing by my kichen tabel. My dog came and zoomd rite into my leg and I flu up into the air and then I landed on the tile on my tummy.

Score 2

This narrative does seem to have a beginning, middle, and end. However, the writer does not reveal her personality or feelings about the event. The final sentence is a run-on, and there are a number of misspelled words (*yers, kichen, tabel, zoomd, rite, flu*).

> At grandmas hous Brewstr knodkd me domn. Brewstr grandma and granpas dogg. I was little. Linsey said it was funny. Brewster lick me. He lick me on my fas. It scare me. but it funny.

Score 1

Although this narrative addresses the prompt, it merits a low score because of pervasive spelling and usage errors, which confuse and seriously detract from the writing.

PROMPT

Write to the mayor or another leader in your community. Thank him or her for what workers, such as firefighters or police, do for the community.

Rubric	4	3	2	1
Focus/Ideas	Reader can understand the letter	Reader can understand part of the letter	Reader cannot understand the letter very well	Reader cannot understand the letter
Organization	Has all the parts of a letter	Has most of the parts of a letter	Missing several parts of a letter	Does not have parts of a letter
Voice	Clearly shows how the writer feels about topic	Shows a little how the writer feels about topic	Does not show very well how the writer feels about topic	Does not show how the writer feels about topic
Word Choice	Uses specific words to explain main idea	Uses some specific words to explain main idea	Words do not help explain main idea	Words are hard to read
Sentences	All sentences clear and complete	Most sentences clear and complete	Some sentences not complete or not clear	Sentences not clear or complete
Conventions	Uses good punctuation and grammar	Uses fair punctuation and grammar	Uses poor punctuation and grammar	Uses very poor punctuation and grammar

645 Lawndale Dr.

Riverside, MO

October 3, 20__

Dear Mr. Willard,

Thank you for keeping Riverside safe. The policemen, firefighters, and crossing guards have done a great job. The policeman comes with the ambulance, or if you need there help. The firefighters put out the fire when there is a fire. The crossing guards help us. They put there stop sign up, and let us walk across the road. Crossing guards always make sure you don't get hurt or hit by a hard car. Thank you so so so much for keeping Riverside safe!

Sincerely,

Trina Hogan

Score 4

This letter expresses very strong feelings; phrases such as "done a great job" and "Thank you so so so much" make the writer's feelings clear. All parts of a letter are included, and all sentences are clear and complete. Conventions are excellent with the exception of a misspelled word (*there* for *their*) in the third and sixth sentences.

August 23, 20__

Dear, Mr. Mayor

Thank you for firefighters! They help us in so many ways. Like they put out fires, rescue people out of fires, get cats out of the tree, and teach children how to be like a firefighter. There was a gas exploshin two miles away from are house! It was good the firefighters put out the fire. I feel grate that there are firefighters.

Love,
Jack P.

Score 3

This letter addresses the prompt and shows just how the writer feels about the topic. The writer uses specific examples of what firefighters do to help. Sentences are clear and complete. A misplaced comma in the greeting, an unnecessary word at the beginning of the third sentence, a missing letter part (the heading), and three misspellings *(exploshin, are* for *our, grate)* do not detract significantly from the letter.

Dear Mrs. Goldsworthy

Officer Hoper came to tell my class about being a Police Officer. She talked about her gun and Peper spray. She let us go in her car. She turnd on the lights and sirin. She tot us about safty. She gave us a sticker, a bracelet, and a pencil. I'm glad Officer Hoper works in Gremantown.

Love Elena

Score 2

This letter explains what one officer did during a visit to a school, but does not thank the community leader or explain what police officers do for the community. The letter is missing a heading as well as commas after the greeting and closing. Sentences are all complete but most begin with "She". A number of misspellings also contribute to the letter's low score.

Dear Mr fiyrFighter,

Thank you for puting out the fiyr. And safing my frend.
You kep us saf. Thank you. Gus

Score 1

This letter addresses a firefighter rather than a community leader. The writer's feelings are clear, but the letter is missing a heading and a closing, and the signature directly follows the last sentence. In addition, there are numerous misspellings that make the piece difficult to read.

PROMPT Write about a place or thing in nature. Describe the place or thing.

Rubric	4	3	2	1
Focus/Ideas	Has a strong main idea and interesting details	Has a main idea and some details	Has a weak main idea and few details	Has no main idea or supporting details
Organization	Strong main idea is supported by facts	Has main idea and a few facts	Main idea and facts are not clear	Does not have facts
Voice	Clearly shows the writer is interested in the topic	Shows the writer is interested in the topic a little	Does not show the writer is interested in the topic very well	Does not show the writer is interested in the topic
Word Choice	Uses specific words to help make ideas clear	Some words help make ideas clear	Words do not help make ideas clear	Words are hard to read
Sentences	Sentences are complete, clear, and not all alike	Sentences are complete and clear	Some sentences are not complete and clear	Sentences not complete or clear
Conventions	Uses good spelling and capitalization	Uses fair spelling and capitalization	Uses poor spelling and capitalization	Uses very poor spelling and capitalization

Jungle

The jungle has many trees and animals. Some animals that live in the jungle are elefants, zebras, monkeys, parrots, gorilla and lions. In the jungle it rains almost every day. The jungle has thowsands of tall trees and plants. There are vines too. Sometimes monkeys swing on vines. Monkeys like climbing trees. Parrots like trees too because they are birds. Elefants and zebras like the ground. They can't go up in trees. Gorillas and lions climb up the trees sometimes and sometimes walk around on the ground. Lions are king of the jungle!

Score 4

This article is focused on the jungle and the plants and animals that can be found there. The writer is interested in the topic and provides a number of details about different jungle animals. Sentences are mostly varied, complete, and clear. There are two misspelled words *(elefants, thowsands)*, and a few missing commas, but they do not interfere with understanding.

Water

Water is really important. Many many things live in water! There are fish, rocks, starfish, sand dollars, sharks, and whales. And there are more fish like angelfish and clownfish. Did you know that water is very very very good for you! We do lots of things with water like, go swimming, go fishing, go boat rideing, you can also surf on the wave! wave! wave! Water is fun and everyone needs water like people and fish.

Score 3

This article is focused on water and its uses and inhabitants. The writer is interested and enthusiastic, and includes a main idea as well as some supporting information. Some specific words are used, such as the names of different sea creatures. There is a run-on sentence. There is also a misspelled word, and some sentences lack appropriate punctuation.

The Beach

The beach has sand and water. Sand is little tiny pieces of rocks. You play in sand. You can make a sandcasel. You can find big rocks. You play frisbey. You can bery people in the san. You can dig a hole. You can see kites and seagulls at the beach. You can step in the water and get wet. The sand by the water gets wet. The sand away doesnt get wet.

Score 2

This article fulfills the prompt. The writer includes details and facts as support. Sentences are clear and complete. However, there is no sense of the writer's personality. There is little variation in sentences, and most begin with *You.* In addition, there are three misspellings and a missing apostrophe.

My dad takes up and we hike. Sometimes my mom goes. She don't like the bugs that much. I don't like miskitos. they itch. I like to sleep in a tent. It's fun, but there is noises. I got scarred one time. It might be a bear.

Score 1

Although this response shows decent control of conventions, it merits a low score because it does not address the prompt. There is no mention of the place in nature that is being written about. The narrative lacks closure.

PROMPT — **Write a story about a boy or a girl who loses something he or she treasures. Tell what happens.**

Rubric	4	3	2	1
Focus/Ideas	Reader can understand the entire story	Reader can understand most of the story	Reader cannot understand the story very well	Reader cannot understand the story
Organization	Has a good beginning, middle, and end	Has a beginning, middle, and end	Events are out of order	Does not have a beginning, middle, and end
Voice	Clearly shows how the writer feels	Shows a little about how the writer feels	Does not show very well how the writer feels	Does not show how the writer feels at all
Word Choice	Has many words that help reader "see" the story	Some words help reader "see" part of the story	Words do not help reader "see" the story	Words are hard to read
Sentences	Sentences complete, clear, and not all alike	Sentences complete and clear	Some sentences not complete or not clear	Sentences not complete or clear
Conventions	Uses good punctuation and grammar	Uses fair punctuation and grammar	Uses poor punctuation and grammar	Uses very poor punctuation and grammar

Henry Got Lost

Once upon a time there was a little white dog named Henry. Every day Henry and his owner Bridget went to the park. They would play catch with a ball, and sometimes a stick. Henry really liked to run fast.

One time, Bridget thro the ball to far. Henry chased the ball. The ball got lost. Henry got lost too. Bridget looked every where but she could not find Henry. He was disappeared! She was sad and scared and she still looked for Henry on her way home. When she got home Henry was sitting by the front door. Bridget was so happy.

Score 4

The story uses well-ordered events to create a clear beginning, middle, and end. The characters and events are realistic and focused on the prompt, and the writer uses transitions *(One time, When)*. Details describe the dog's appearance and actions, as well as Bridget's feelings. There are a few spelling errors and an error in verb use *(He was disappeared!)*, but they do not interfere with meaning.

Lost and Found

One day a little boy was playing with his favorite toy. His mom asked him if he wanted to go to the store with her. He said yes. He got his stuff and they left. At the store they bot lemons, apples, grapes, and lots of other things.

When they got home the boy ran strate to the living room to play with his toy and . . . it wasn't there!!! The boy looked under the table, in his bed, and on the couch. Then he went to bed crying and when he was aslepp his mom found it in the blanket corner. When he woke up he was releaved the toy was there!!!!

Score 3

The events are in a logical order, creating a clear beginning, middle, and end. The writer uses some transitions (*One day, When*) to help clarify events. Most sentences focus on the topic. Some details about the toy's loss are given, but details about what the boy and his mother bought at the store are unnecessary. More descriptive detail would make the story more interesting. There are a few misspellings, but most sentences are correctly capitalized and punctuated.

Boomer and baby

One time there was a boy named Luke that had two cats.

There name was boomer and baby. He loved thim so much.

Boomer was orange and baby was black. Boomer had green

eyes baby had brown eye. They wer his first cats he new.

He was sad whin they died.

Score 2

The story follows the prompt to a degree, but focuses on the cats rather than the boy's loss. Descriptive details are given about the cats, but little other detail. There are errors in spelling, capitalization, subject-verb agreement, and sentence construction.

the Dog

Its Chasing His tal

the dog is Runing

the Dog is Jumping

the Dog is Climbing

Score 1

This writing sample does not have a beginning, middle, and end. There are no events, just a list of activities the dog does. There is no sense of the writer. The structure of sentences is repetitive and simple. There is at least one error in each sentence, although no mistakes interfere with the reader's understanding.

PROMPT **Write a report about an inventor or an invention. Find facts about your topic in books or magazines or on the Internet.**

Rubric	4	3	2	1
Focus/Ideas	Reader learns many facts about the topic	Reader learns some facts about the topic	Reader learns few facts about the topic	Reader learns nothing about the topic
Organization	Facts organized in paragraphs	Facts mostly organized in paragraphs	Some facts organized in paragraphs	Facts not organized
Voice	Clearly shows that writer knows the topic	Shows a little that writer knows the topic	Does not show very well that writer knows the topic	Does not show that the writer knows the topic
Word Choice	Uses specific words to tell about the topic	Uses some specific words to tell about the topic	Uses few specific words to tell about the topic	No specific words to tell about the topic
Sentences	Sentences complete, clear, and not all alike	Sentences complete and clear	Some sentences not complete or not clear	Sentences not complete or clear
Conventions	Uses good spelling and capitalization	Uses fair spelling and capitalization	Uses poor spelling and capitalization	Uses very poor spelling and capitalization

Zip!

In the 1890s, shoes had many tiny buttons on them. Whitcomb L. Judson had an idea. He made the clasp locker for shoes, but it didn't work very well.

In 1913 Gideon Sundback had an idea. He made the clasp locker work better. He called it the Hookless 2. People didn't buy it though.

In 1921 the B. F. Goodrich Company put the Hookless 2 on their rain boots. Mr. Goodrich called it the zipper. That was the sound it made. Zip! This time the invention became popular. Now zippers are everywhere! Zip! Zip!

Score 4

Report sticks to the topic and gives many facts. Information is presented in time order. The report is interesting and well researched. A variety of sentences (a compound sentence and an exclamatory sentence) adds interest. Grammar, capitalization, and spelling are all excellent.

Leonardo da Vinci was a famous inventor. He was born on April 15, 1452, in a village in Italy called Vinci. Leonardo's name means Leonardo from Vinci. Leonardo mirror writed because he was left-handed. Mirror writing is writing right to left and backwards.

Leonardo da Vinci was a artist. He painted two famous paintings called the Mona Lisa and The Last Supper. He also invented a parachute in the shape of a peramid. Leonardo da Vinci died May 2, 1597. He was 67.

Score 3

This report includes interesting information and organizes it well. Voice is knowledgeable. Word choice is precise and the writer defines a term *(Mirror writing is writing right to left and backwards.).* Though a number begin with *Leonardo* or *He*, sentences are generally smooth and well constructed. A verb error *(writed)* and a misspelling *(peramid),* as well as an incorrect article *(a artist)* detract somewhat from the report.

Hershey History

The mans name who created the Hershey bar was Milton S. Hershey. At first he made carmal, not chocolate. Then he started making chocolate covered carmals. After that he made hershey bars. When he created them he moved back to the town were he was born. Right now its called Hershey, Pennsylvania.

Score 2

This report is focused and supported with some details. Information is generally organized by sequence and uses some specific words to tell about the topic. Sentence and punctuation errors, lack of capitalization, and misspellings *(mans, carmal, hershey, its)* detract from the report.

Hula Hoops

The kids in Ejipt played with hoops. They maked them of vines. They rolled them. Then someone maked them of plastek. They seld them they maked lots of monee.

Score 1

Ideas are sometimes unclear or undeveloped. Sentences are choppy, and many begin with they. A run-on sentence, incorrect verb forms *(maked, seld)*, no paragraph indention, and misspellings *(Ejipt, plastek, monee)* seriously detract from the report.

Weekly Rubrics

Rubric	6	5	4	3	2	1
Focus/Ideas	Focused narrative about the chosen pet, with story action	Narrative includes some story action	Fair narrative about the chosen pet, with some details	Generally focused narrative about the chosen pet, with few details	Narrative includes few details	Unclear writing with no details
Organization	Strong beginning, middle, and end	Fairly strong beginning, middle, and end	Clear beginning, middle, and end	Recognizable beginning, middle, and end	Little direction from beginning to end	Lacks beginning, middle, and end
Voice	Clearly shows how writer feels about topic	Feelings are clear and apparent	Shows some feeling toward topic	Feelings about topic unclear	Needs to show more feeling about topic	Shows no feeling about topic
Word Choice	Vivid, precise words	Vivid words	Clear words	Clear language attempted	Adequate but lacks vivid or clear words	Vague or misused words
Sentences	All sentences clear and complete	Most sentences clear and complete	Many sentences clear and complete	Some sentences clear and complete	Few sentences complete	Many incomplete or unclear sentences
Conventions	All sentences begin with uppercase letters and end with periods	Many sentences begin with uppercase letters and end with periods	Some sentences begin with uppercase letters and end with periods	Few sentences begin with uppercase letters and end with periods	Several sentences are missing uppercase letters and periods	Many errors in capitalization and use of periods

Rubric	5	4	3	2	1
Focus/Ideas	Focused narrative about the chosen pet, with story action	Good narrative about the chosen pet, with some details	Generally focused narrative about the chosen pet, with few details	Narrative includes few details	Unclear writing with no details
Organization	Strong beginning, middle, and end	Clear beginning, middle, and end	Recognizable beginning, middle, and end	Little direction from beginning to end	Lacks beginning, middle, and end
Voice	Clearly shows how writer feels about topic	Shows some feeling toward topic	Feelings about topic unclear	Needs to show more feeling about topic	Shows no feeling about topic
Word Choice	Vivid, precise words	Clear words	Clear language attempted	Adequate but lacks vivid or clear words	Vague or misused words
Sentences	All sentences clear and complete	Most sentences clear and complete	Many sentences clear and complete	Some sentences complete	Many incomplete or unclear sentences
Conventions	All sentences begin with uppercase letters and end with periods	Most sentences begin with uppercase letters and end with periods	Some sentences begin with uppercase letters and end with periods	Several sentences are missing uppercase letters and periods	Many errors in capitalization and use of periods

Rubric	4	3	2	1
Focus/Ideas	Focused narrative about the chosen pet, with story action	Good narrative about the chosen pet, with some details	Generally focused narrative about a pet, with few details	Unclear writing with no details
Organization	Strong beginning, middle, and end	Recognizable beginning, middle, and end	Little direction from beginning to end	Lacks beginning, middle, and end
Voice	Clearly shows how writer feels about topic	Shows some feeling toward topic	Needs to show more feeling about topic	Shows no feeling about topic
Word Choice	Vivid, precise words	Clear words	Adequate but lacks vivid or clear words	Vague or misused words
Sentences	All sentences clear and complete	Most sentences clear and complete	Some sentences complete	Many incomplete or unclear sentences
Conventions	All sentences begin with uppercase letters and end with periods	Most sentences begin with uppercase letters and end with periods	Several sentences are missing uppercase letters and periods	Many errors in capitalization and use of periods

Rubric	6	5	4	3	2	1
Focus/Ideas	Imaginative story about a person and animal, with fantasy element	Excellent narrative about a person and animal includes fantasy element	Good narrative about a person and animal, with fantasy element	Generally focused narrative about a person and animal	Unfocused narrative about a person and animal	Unclear writing with no details or fantasy element
Organization	Has beginning, middle, and end, and a related picture	Has beginning, middle, end, and picture	Clear beginning, middle, and end	Recognizable beginning, middle, and end	Hard to recognize beginning, middle, end, or art	Lacks beginning, middle, and end
Voice	Writer's imagination and feelings about topic are clear	Writer's feelings about topic are clear	Good writer involvement	Writer's imagination clear	Writer's imagination and involvement not very clear	Little evidence of imagination or involvement
Word Choice	Vivid, precise words	Clear, descriptive language used	Precise words	Clear words	Adequate but lacks vivid or clear words	Vague or misused words
Sentences	Every sentence has a subject	Most sentences have a subject	Few sentences incomplete; many sentences have a subject	Some incomplete sentences	Several incomplete sentences	Most or all sentences are incomplete
Conventions	No errors in capitalization and punctuation	Few errors in capitalization and punctuation	Some errors in capitalization and punctuation	Some errors affect understanding	Many errors that affect understanding	Serious errors that prevent understanding

Rubric	5	4	3	2	1
Focus/Ideas	Imaginative story about a person and animal, with fantasy element	Good narrative about a person and animal, with fantasy element	Generally focused narrative about a person and animal	Unfocused narrative about a person and animal	Unclear writing with no details or fantasy element
Organization	Has beginning, middle, and end, and a related picture	Has beginning, middle, end, and picture	Recognizable beginning, middle, and end	Hard to recognize beginning, middle, and end or art	Lacks beginning, middle, and end
Voice	Writer's imagination and feelings about topic are clear	Writer's feelings about topic are clear	Writer imagination clear	Writer imagination and involvement not very clear	Little evidence of imagination or involvement
Word Choice	Vivid, precise words	Clear words	Some clear words	Adequate but lacks vivid or clear words	Vague or misused words
Sentences	Every sentence has a subject	Most sentences have a subject	Some incomplete sentences	Several incomplete sentences	Most or all sentences are incomplete
Conventions	Few or no errors in capitalization and punctuation	No serious errors in capitalization and punctuation	Few errors affect understanding	Some errors that affect understanding	Serious errors that prevent understanding

Rubric	4	3	2	1
Focus/Ideas	Imaginative story about a person and animal, with fantasy element	Good narrative about a person and animal, with fantasy element	Generally focused narrative about a person and animal	Unclear writing with no details or fantasy element
Organization	Has beginning, middle, and end and a related picture	Has beginning, middle, end, and picture	Hard to recognize beginning, middle, and end or art	Lacks beginning, middle, and end
Voice	Writer's imagination and feelings about topic are clear	Writer's feelings about topic are clear	Writer imagination and involvement not very clear	Little evidence of imagination or involvement
Word Choice	Vivid, precise words	Clear words	Adequate but lacks vivid or clear words	Vague or misused words
Sentences	Every sentence has a subject	Most sentences have a subject	Several incomplete sentences	Most or all sentences are incomplete
Conventions	Few or no errors in capitalization and punctuation	No serious errors in capitalization and punctuation	Some errors that affect understanding	Serious errors that prevent understanding

Rubric	6	5	4	3	2	1
Focus/Ideas	Poem with strong focus on a kind of animal and sensory details	Poem focused on one kind of animal or sensory details	Poem with clear focus on a kind of animal; some sensory details	Poem focused and supported with sensory details	Poem with weak focus on sensory details or feelings	Rambling lines with no clear topic or details; not a poem
Organization	Carefully organized in lines, with understandable description	Organized in lines; contains description	Organized in lines	Organized in lines at times	Not consistently arranged in lines	Little or no recognizable arrangement
Voice	Imaginative and original, showing observed or imagined details	Mostly imaginative and original; expresses some feelings	Shows imagined or observed details	At times imaginative and descriptive	Somewhat descriptive; not original	Not imaginative, descriptive, or original
Word Choice	Vivid descriptive words and rhyming words; expresses feelings	Language expresses writer's feelings	Some vivid descriptive words and rhyming words	Uses few descriptive and rhyming words	Little use of vivid words or rhyming words	Dull, vague, or incorrect words
Sentences	Clear sentences with subjects and predicates	Mostly clear sentences with subjects and predicates	Fairly clear sentences with subjects and predicates	Some unclear sentences or incomplete predicates	Many unclear sentences or incomplete predicates	Incoherent or incorrect sentences
Conventions	Correct capitalization and predicates	Mostly correct capitalization and predicates	Some correct capitalization and predicates	Many errors; do not affect understanding of poem	Enough errors to affect understanding of poem	Many errors prevent understanding of poem

Rubric	5	4	3	2	1
Focus/Ideas	Poem with strong focus on a kind of animal and sensory details	Poem with clear focus on a kind of animal; some sensory details	Poem focused and supported with sensory details	Poem with weak focus on sensory details or feelings	Rambling lines with no clear topic or details; not a poem
Organization	Carefully organized in lines, with understandable description	Organized in lines; contains description	Organized in lines	Not consistently arranged in lines	Little or no recognizable arrangement
Voice	Imaginative and original, showing observed or imagined details	Mostly imaginative and original; expresses some feelings	At times imaginative and descriptive	Somewhat descriptive; not original	Not imaginative, descriptive, or original
Word Choice	Vivid descriptive words and rhyming words; expresses feelings	Some vivid descriptive words and rhyming words	Uses few descriptive and rhyming words	Little use of vivid words or rhyming words	Dull, vague, or incorrect words
Sentences	Clear sentences with subjects and predicates	Mostly clear sentences with subjects and predicates	Some unclear sentences or incomplete predicates	Many unclear sentences or incomplete predicates	Incoherent or incorrect sentences
Conventions	Correct capitalization and predicates	Mostly correct capitalization and predicates	Many errors; do not affect understanding of poem	Enough errors to affect understanding of poem	Many errors prevent understanding of poem

Rubric	4	3	2	1
Focus/Ideas	Poem with strong focus on a kind of animal and sensory details	Poem with clear focus on a kind of animal; some sensory details	Poem with weak focus on sensory details or feelings	Rambling lines with no clear topic or details; not a poem
Organization	Carefully organized in lines, with understandable description	Organized in lines; contains description	Not consistently arranged in lines	Little or no recognizable arrangement
Voice	Imaginative and original, showing observed or imagined details	Mostly imaginative and original; expresses some feelings	Somewhat imaginative; not original	Not imaginative, descriptive, or original
Word Choice	Vivid descriptive words and rhyming words; expresses feelings	Some vivid descriptive words and rhyming words	Little use of vivid words or rhyming words	Dull, vague, or incorrect words
Sentences	Clear sentences with subjects and predicates	Mostly clear sentences with subjects and predicates	Several unclear sentences or incomplete predicates	Incoherent or incorrect sentences
Conventions	Correct capitalization and predicates	Mostly correct capitalization and predicates	Enough errors to affect understanding of poem	Many errors prevent understanding of poem

Rubric	6	5	4	3	2	1
Focus/Ideas	Excellent personal narrative; strong details show what writer saw	Good personal narrative; many good details of what the writer saw	Fair personal narrative; some good details	Narrative's topic is clear	Personal narrative not clearly about the topic; few details	Little or no focus on self or animals in narrative; no clear details
Organization	Well-developed beginning, middle, and end; words in sensible order	Most events in clear beginning, middle, and end	Identifiable beginning, middle, and end; words in order	Events begin to be told in recognizable order	Events told out of order or words without sensible order	Events and words in no logical sequence
Voice	Clearly shows how writer feels about observed events	Writer's feelings apparent	Some glimpses of writer's feelings about topic	Limited view of writer's feelings	Does not show how writer feels about observed events	No sense of writer's self in the composition
Word Choice	Appropriate words about self and animals make sense	Descriptive language about self and animals	Some clear words about self and animals	Few clear words about topic	Unclear words about the topic	Words are hard to understand
Sentences	All sentences clear and complete	Most sentences clear and complete	Many sentences clear and complete	Some sentences clear and complete	Some sentences incomplete	Many incomplete or unclear sentences
Conventions	All sentences begin with uppercase letters and end with periods	Most sentences begin with uppercase letters and end with periods	Some sentences begin with uppercase letters and end with periods	Few sentences are missing uppercase letters or periods	Several sentences are missing uppercase letters or periods	Many errors in capitalization and use of periods

Rubric	5	4	3	2	1
Focus/Ideas	Excellent personal narrative; strong details show what writer saw	Good personal narrative; some good details of what writer saw	Narrative's topic is clear	Personal narrative not clearly about the topic; few details	Little or no focus on self or animals in narrative; no clear details
Organization	Well-developed beginning, middle, and end; words in sensible order	Identifiable beginning, middle, and end; words in order	Events begin to be told in recognizable order	Events told out of order or words without sensible order	Events and words in no logical sequence
Voice	Clearly shows how writer feels about observed events	Some glimpses of writer's feelings about topic	Limited view of writer's feelings	Does not show how writer feels about observed events	No sense of writer's self in the composition
Word Choice	Appropriate words about self and animals make sense	Some clear words about self and animals	Few clear words about topic	Unclear words about the topic	Words are hard to understand
Sentences	All sentences clear and complete	Most sentences clear and complete	Some sentences clear and complete	Some sentences complete	Many incomplete or unclear sentences
Conventions	All sentences begin with uppercase letters and end with periods	Most sentences begin with uppercase letters and end with periods	Few sentences are missing uppercase letters or periods	Several sentences are missing uppercase letters or periods	Many errors in capitalization and use of periods

Rubric	4	3	2	1
Focus/Ideas	Excellent personal narrative; strong details show what writer saw	Good personal narrative; some good details of what writer saw	Personal narrative not clearly about the topic; few details	Little or no focus on self or animals in narrative; no clear details
Organization	Well-developed beginning, middle, and end; words in sensible order	Identifiable beginning, middle, and end; words in order	Events told out of order or words without sensible order	Events and words in no logical sequence
Voice	Clearly shows how writer feels about observed events	Some glimpses of writer's feelings about topic	Does not show how writer feels about observed events	No sense of writer's self in the composition
Word Choice	Appropriate words about self and animals make sense	Some clear words about self and animals	Unclear words about the topic	Words are hard to understand
Sentences	All sentences clear and complete	Most sentences clear and complete	Some sentences complete	Many incomplete or unclear sentences
Conventions	All sentences begin with uppercase letters and end with periods	Most sentences begin with uppercase letters and end with periods	Several sentences are missing uppercase letters or periods	Many errors in capitalization and use of periods

Rubric	6	5	4	3	2	1
Focus/Ideas	Focused narrative with clear events that could really happen	Generally focused narrative with events that could happen	Fairly focused narrative; most events realistic	Narrative has weak focus; few events are realistic	Narrative not clearly focused throughout; events not realistic	Narrative with no focus; no realistic events
Organization	Sentences are in order, from beginning to middle to end	Most sentences are in order, from beginning to middle to end	Many sentences are in order, beginning to middle to end	Few sentences are in order; some parts are weak	Sentences are not in order; weak middle or ending	Order of ideas unclear
Voice	Writer's interest is very evident and engages reader	Writer's interest in story is very evident	Writer's interest in story is evident	Writer's voice sometimes evident	Writer's interest in story is not very evident	Writing shows little interest
Word Choice	Vivid, precise words bring story to life	Includes language that makes story believable	Language makes story fairly lively	Clear and appropriate word choice	Language is adequate	Vague, dull, or misused words
Sentences	All sentences clear and complete	Most sentences clear and complete	Some sentences clear and complete	Few incomplete or run-on sentences	Some incomplete or run-on sentences	Many incomplete or run-on sentences
Conventions	All sentences capitalized and punctuated correctly	Most sentences are capitalized and punctuated correctly	Some sentences are capitalized and punctuated correctly; few errors	Many errors in capitalization and end punctuation	A number of mistakes in capitalization and end punctuation	Capitalization and punctuation mistakes prevent understanding

Rubric	5	4	3	2	1
Focus/Ideas	Focused narrative with clear events that could really happen	Generally focused narrative with events that could happen	Fairly focused narrative; most events realistic	Narrative not clearly focused throughout; events not realistic	Narrative with no focus; no realistic events
Organization	Sentences are in order, from beginning to middle to end	Most sentences are in order, beginning to middle to end	Some sentences are in order; some parts are weak	Sentences are not in order; weak middle or ending	Order of ideas unclear
Voice	Writer's interest in story is very evident	Writer's interest in story is evident	Writer's interest in story sometimes evident	Writer's interest in story is not very evident	Writing shows little interest
Word Choice	Vivid, precise words bring story to life	Language makes story fairly lively	Clear and appropriate word choice	Language is adequate	Vague, dull, or misused words
Sentences	All sentences clear and complete	Most sentences clear and complete	Few incomplete or run-on sentences	Some incomplete or run-on sentences	Many incomplete or run-on sentences
Conventions	All sentences capitalized and punctuated correctly	Most sentences are capitalized and punctuated correctly	Some errors in capitalization and end punctuation	A number of mistakes in capitalization and end punctuation	Capitalization and punctuation mistakes prevent understanding

Rubric	4	3	2	1
Focus/Ideas	Focused narrative with clear events that could really happen	Generally focused narrative with events that could happen	Narrative not clearly focused throughout; events not realistic	Narrative with no focus; no realistic events
Organization	Sentences are in order, from beginning to middle to end	Most sentences are in order, beginning to middle to end	Sentences are not in order; weak middle or ending	Order of ideas unclear
Voice	Writer's interest in story is very evident	Writer's interest in story is evident	Writer's interest in story is not very evident	Writing shows little interest
Word Choice	Vivid, precise words bring story to life	Clear words make story fairly lively	Language is adequate	Vague, dull, or misused words
Sentences	All sentences clear and complete	Most sentences clear and complete	Some incomplete or run-on sentences	Many incomplete or run-on sentences
Conventions	All sentences capitalized and punctuated correctly	Most sentences are capitalized and punctuated correctly	A number of mistakes in capitalization and end punctuation	Capitalization and punctuation mistakes prevent understanding

Rubric	6	5	4	3	2	1
Focus/Ideas	Clear and focused composition on one topic and tells about real people and things	Composition focuses on one topic and tells about real people and things most of the time	Generally focuses on topic and tells about real people and things	Attempts to stay on topic and generally tells about real people and things	Shows difficulty staying on topic; may seem like fiction	Topic is unclear; does not tell about real people or things
Organization	Tells ideas clearly in a sensible order	Tells ideas in a sensible order	Tells ideas in a fairly sensible order	Many ideas told in sensible order	Includes ideas but not in sensible order	Sentences and order hard to understand
Voice	Expresses ideas in interesting ways	Expresses ideas in interesting ways	Expresses interest in topic	Writer's interest in topic sometimes evident	Does not show writer's interest in topic	Lacks involvement in topic
Word Choice	Uses clear, vivid words about the topic, wild animals	Uses clear language most of the time	Uses clear words, with exceptions	Words are appropriate to topic	Some words are unclear or do not fit topic	Many words are unclear or do not fit topic
Sentences	Each sentence is complete and expresses one idea	Most sentences are complete and express one idea	Many sentences are complete and express one idea	Few sentences are complete	Some sentences are incomplete or unclear	Sentences are incomplete or unclear
Conventions	All sentences have correct end punctuation	Most sentences have correct end punctuation	Many sentences have correct end punctuation	Few sentences have incorrect end punctuation	Several sentences have incorrect end punctuation	Sentences have incorrect end punctuation

Rubric	5	4	3	2	1
Focus/Ideas	Focuses on one topic and tells about real people and things	Generally focuses on topic and tells about real people and things	Attempts to stay on topic and generally tells about real people and things	Shows difficulty staying on topic; may seem like fiction	Topic is unclear; does not tell about real people or things
Organization	Tells ideas clearly in a sensible order	Tells ideas in a sensible order	Many ideas told in sensible order	Includes ideas but not in sensible order	Sentences and order hard to understand
Voice	Expresses ideas in interesting ways	Expresses ideas clearly	Writer's interest in topic evident	Does not show writer's interest in topic	Lacks involvement in topic
Word Choice	Uses clear words about the topic, wild animals	Uses clear words, with exceptions	Words are appropriate to topic	Some words are unclear or do not fit topic	Many words are unclear or do not fit topic
Sentences	Each sentence is complete and expresses one idea	Most sentences are complete and express one idea	Few sentences are complete or express one idea	Some sentences are incomplete or unclear	Sentences are incomplete or unclear
Conventions	All sentences have correct end punctuation	Most sentences have correct end punctuation	Few sentences have incorrect end punctuation	Several sentences have incorrect end punctuation	Sentences have incorrect end punctuation

Rubric	4	3	2	1
Focus/Ideas	Focuses on one topic and tells about real people and things	Generally focuses on topic and tells about real people and things	Shows difficulty staying on topic; may seem like fiction	Topic is unclear; does not tell about real people or things
Organization	Tells ideas clearly in a sensible order	Tells ideas in a sensible order	Includes ideas but not in sensible order	Sentences and order hard to understand
Voice	Expresses ideas in interesting ways	Expresses ideas clearly	Does not show writer's interest in topic	Lacks involvement in topic
Word Choice	Uses clear words about the topic, wild animals	Uses clear words, with exceptions	Some words are unclear or do not fit topic	Many words are unclear or do not fit topic
Sentences	Each sentence is complete and expresses one idea	Most sentences are complete and express one idea	Some sentences are incomplete or unclear	Sentences are incomplete or unclear
Conventions	All sentences have correct end punctuation	Most sentences have correct end punctuation	Several sentences have incorrect end punctuation	Sentences have incorrect end punctuation

Rubric	6	5	4	3	2	1
Focus/Ideas	Strong persuasive letter with clear, convincing reasons	Good persuasive letter; some clear, convincing reasons	Persuasive letter with some convincing reasons	Persuasive letter with one or two convincing reasons	Letter often off topic; needs more convincing reasons	Letter lacks focus and reasons that persuade
Organization	Has greeting, date, sentences in a sensible order, closing, and signature	Has greeting, date, sentences in a reasonable order, closing, and signature	One letter part missing	One letter part missing and sentences out of order	More than one letter part missing; sentences in no apparent order	Letter parts missing; few sentences, in no apparent order
Voice	Strongly expresses writer's feelings and ideas in friendly voice	Mostly expresses writer's feelings and ideas in friendly voice	Generally expresses writer's feelings or ideas in friendly voice	Hardly expresses feelings or friendly voice	Hardly expresses feelings and friendly voice	Lacks feelings, friendly voice, and writer's interest
Word Choice	Uses words to persuade effectively	Some words to persuade used effectively	Includes several words to persuade	Few words used to persuade	Limited word choice; no words that persuade	Dull words; no words that persuade
Sentences	Complete and varied sentences	Complete sentences; some variety	Mostly complete sentences; little variety	Generally complete sentences; little variety	Some incomplete or unclear sentences	Incomplete and unclear sentences
Conventions	Uses common nouns correctly; no mistakes	Uses common nouns correctly; no serious mistakes	Uses common nouns correctly; some mistakes	Some nouns used incorrectly; many mistakes	Most nouns used incorrectly; many mistakes	Many serious mistakes hinder understanding

Rubric	5	4	3	2	1
Focus/Ideas	Strong persuasive letter with clear, convincing reasons	Good persuasive letter; some clear, convincing reasons	Persuasive letter with some convincing reasons	Persuasive letter with one or two convincing reasons	Letter lacks focus and reasons that persuade
Organization	Has greeting, date, sentences in a sensible order, closing, and signature	Has greeting, date, sentences in a reasonable order, closing, and signature	One letter part missing, or sentences in no apparent order	One letter part missing and sentences in no apparent order	Letter parts missing; few sentences, in no apparent order
Voice	Strongly expresses writer's feelings and ideas in friendly voice	Mostly expresses writer's feelings and ideas in friendly voice	Generally expresses writer's feelings or ideas in friendly voice	Hardly expresses feelings or friendly voice	Lacks feelings, friendly voice, and writer's interest
Word Choice	Uses words to persuade effectively	Some words to persuade used effectively	Includes several words to persuade	Few words used to persuade	Dull words; no words that persuade
Sentences	Complete and varied sentences	Complete sentences; some variety	Mostly complete sentences; little variety	Generally complete sentences; little variety	Incomplete and unclear sentences
Conventions	Uses common nouns correctly; no mistakes	Uses common nouns correctly; no serious mistakes	Uses common nouns correctly; some mistakes	Some nouns used incorrectly; many mistakes	Many serious mistakes hinder understanding

Rubric	4	3	2	1
Focus/Ideas	Strong persuasive letter with clear, convincing reasons	Good persuasive letter with some clear, convincing reasons	Persuasive letter drifts from topic; needs stronger reasons	Letter lacks focus and reasons that persuade
Organization	Has greeting, sentences in a sensible order, closing, and signature	Has greeting, sentences in reasonable order, closing, and signature	One or more letter parts missing; sentences in no apparent order	Letter parts missing; few sentences, in no apparent order
Voice	Strongly expresses writer's feelings and ideas in friendly voice	Expresses writer's feelings or ideas in friendly voice	Hardly expresses feelings or friendly voice	Lacks feelings, friendly voice, and writer's interest
Word Choice	Uses words to persuade effectively	Some words to persuade used effectively	Little word choice; few words that persuade	No words that persuade
Sentences	Complete and varied sentences	Complete sentences; some variety	Some incomplete or unclear sentences	Incomplete and unclear sentences
Conventions	Uses common nouns correctly; no mistakes or few mistakes	Uses common nouns correctly; no serious mistakes	Many mistakes; some nouns used incorrectly	Many serious mistakes hinder understanding

Rubric	6	5	4	3	2	1
Focus/Ideas	Focuses on one topic; interesting facts about real people and things	Focuses on one topic; facts about real people and things	Somewhat focuses on topic and tells some clear facts	Somewhat focuses on topic or tells some clear facts	Shows difficulty staying on topic; needs clearer facts	Does not stay on topic; lacks factual content
Organization	Tells facts and ideas clearly in a sensible order	Tells facts and ideas in a sensible order	Most facts and ideas are in order	Some facts and ideas are in order	Facts and ideas not in sensible order	Jumbles ideas
Voice	Expresses writer's ideas in interesting ways	Expresses ideas in fairly interesting ways	Expresses ideas with some interest	Expresses ideas with little interest	Does not show much interest in topic	Does not show interest in topic
Word Choice	Uses clear words including at least one proper noun	Uses clear words, with exceptions; has a proper noun	Most words are used clearly; has a proper noun	Some words are used clearly; has a proper noun	Some words are unclear.or do not fit topic	Words are unclear or do not fit topic
Sentences	Each sentence is complete; sentences are varied	Most sentences are complete	Some sentences are complete	Some sentences are unclear	Some sentences are incomplete and unclear	Sentences are incomplete or unclear
Conventions	Capitalization and end punctuation are correct	Few errors in capitalization or end punctuation	Some errors in capitalization or end punctuation	Many errors in capitalization or end punctuation	Numerous capitalization or punctuation errors	Most or all sentences missing punctuation and capitalization

Rubric	5	4	3	2	1
Focus/Ideas	Focuses on one topic; interesting facts about real people and things	Generally focuses on topic and tells about real people and things	Somewhat focuses on topic and tells some clear facts	Shows difficulty staying on topic; needs clearer facts	Does not stay on topic; lacks factual content
Organization	Tells facts and ideas clearly in a sensible order	Tells facts and ideas in a sensible order	Some facts and ideas are in order	Facts and ideas not in sensible order	Jumbles ideas
Voice	Expresses writer's ideas in interesting ways	Expresses ideas in fairly interesting ways	Expresses ideas with little interest	Does not show much interest in topic	Does not show interest in topic
Word Choice	Uses clear words including at least one proper noun	Uses clear words, with exceptions; has a proper noun	Most words are used clearly; has a proper noun	Some words are unclear or do not fit topic	Words are unclear or do not fit topic
Sentences	Each sentence is complete; sentences are varied	Most sentences are complete	Some sentences are complete	Some sentences are incomplete or unclear	Sentences are incomplete or unclear
Conventions	Capitalization and end punctuation are correct	Few errors in capitalization or end punctuation	Some errors in capitalization or end punctuation	Several sentences have capitalization or punctuation errors	Many errors; proper noun missing or not capitalized

Rubric	4	3	2	1
Focus/Ideas	Focuses on one topic; interesting facts about real people and things	Generally focuses on topic and tells about real people and things	Shows difficulty staying on topic; needs clearer facts	Does not stay on topic; lacks factual content
Organization	Tells facts and ideas clearly in a sensible order	Tells facts and ideas in a sensible order	Facts and ideas not in sensible order	Jumbles ideas
Voice	Expresses writer's ideas in interesting ways	Expresses ideas in fairly interesting ways	Does not show much interest in topic	Does not show interest in topic
Word Choice	Uses clear words including at least one proper noun	Uses clear words, with exceptions; has a proper noun	Some words are unclear or do not fit topic	Words are unclear or do not fit topic
Sentences	Each sentence is complete; sentences are varied	Most sentences are complete	Some sentences are incomplete or unclear	Sentences are incomplete or unclear
Conventions	Capitalization and end punctuation are correct	Few errors in capitalization or end punctuation	Several sentences have capitalization or punctuation errors	Many errors; proper noun missing or not capitalized

Rubric	6	5	4	3	2	1
Focus/Ideas	Clearly helps reader understand people and ideas; strong details	Helps reader understand people and ideas; strong details	Helps reader understand people and ideas; uses some details	Sometimes helps reader understand people and ideas; sometimes uses details	Attempts to explain people and ideas; few details	Does not explain people or ideas; no supporting details
Organization	Main ideas and details in clear, logical order	Main ideas and details in logical order	Ideas and details in understandable order	Most ideas and details in reasonable order	Ideas and details not well organized	Ideas and details missing or not organized
Voice	Clearly expresses writer's interest and ideas	Expresses writer's interest and ideas	Writer's interest and ideas presented	Writer's interest not always evident	Little sense of writer's interest or ideas	Does not express writer's interest and ideas
Word Choice	Many vivid and exact words about the topic	Sufficient use of vivid or exact words	Some vivid and exact words	A few vivid and exact words	Words about the topic rarely vivid	Dull, vague, or incorrect words
Sentences	All sentences complete and clear	Most sentences complete and clear	Sentences generally complete and clear	Some sentences incomplete or unclear	Most sentences incomplete or unclear	Sentences incomplete, unclear
Conventions	No errors; personal title(s) capitalized and punctuated	Few errors; personal title(s) capitalized and punctuated	Not many errors; personal title(s) capitalized and punctuated	Few errors prevent understanding; some personal titles capitalized	Errors affect understanding; personal titles not capitalized	Serious errors prevent understanding

Rubric	5	4	3	2	1
Focus/Ideas	Clearly helps reader understand people and ideas; strong details	Helps reader understand people and ideas; uses details	Sometimes helps reader understand people and ideas; sometimes uses details	Attempts to explain people and ideas; few details	Does not explain people or ideas; no supporting details
Organization	Main idea and details in clear, logical order	Ideas and details in logical order	Some ideas and details in logical order	Ideas and details not well organized	Ideas and details missing or not organized
Voice	Clearly expresses writer's interest and ideas	Expresses writer's interest and ideas	Writer's interest expressed at times	Little sense of writer's interest or ideas	Does not express writer's interest and ideas
Word Choice	Many vivid or exact words about the topic	Some vivid and exact words about the topic	A few vivid and exact words about the topic	Words about the topic rarely vivid	Dull, vague, or incorrect words
Sentences	All sentences complete and clear	Most sentences complete and clear	Some sentences incomplete or unclear	Most sentences incomplete or unclear	Sentences incomplete, unclear
Conventions	Few or no errors; personal title(s) capitalized and punctuated	Not many errors; personal title(s) capitalized and punctuated	Few errors prevent understanding; some personal titles capitalized	Errors affect understanding; personal titles not capitalized	Serious errors prevent understanding

Rubric	4	3	2	1
Focus/Ideas	Clearly helps reader understand people and ideas; strong details	Helps reader understand people and ideas; uses details	Attempts to explain people and ideas; few details	Does not explain people or ideas; no supporting details
Organization	Main idea and details in clear, logical order	Ideas and details in logical order	Ideas and details not well organized	Ideas and details missing or not organized
Voice	Clearly expresses writer's interest and ideas	Expresses writer's interest and ideas	Little sense of writer's interest or ideas	Does not express writer's interest and ideas
Word Choice	Many vivid or exact words about the topic	Some vivid and exact words about the topic	Few vivid or exact words about the topic	Dull, vague, or incorrect words
Sentences	All sentences complete and clear	Most sentences complete and clear	Most sentences incomplete or unclear	Sentences incomplete, unclear
Conventions	Few or no errors; personal title(s) capitalized and punctuated	Not many errors; personal title(s) capitalized and punctuated	Errors affect understanding; personal titles not capitalized	Serious errors prevent understanding

POEM

Rubric	6	5	4	3	2	1
Focus/Ideas	Strong focus on chosen topic; describes action	Clear focus on chosen topic; describes action well	Poem generally focused; clear description about action	Unclear focus; some clear description	Weak focus on chosen topic; needs clearer description	Rambling lines on unclear topic; not a poem
Organization	Short poetic lines describe event in understandable sequence	Short poetic lines describe event in sequence	Most poetic lines are told in sequence	Some lines organized in sequence	Lines do not describe event in sequence	No recognizable sequence or arrangement
Voice	Imaginative and original	Mostly imaginative, original	At times original and imaginative	Little imagination	Tries to be imaginative; not original	Not imaginative or original
Word Choice	Well-chosen, vivid words and rhyming words	Some well-chosen, vivid words and rhyming words	Vivid and rhyming words attempted	Weak language	Little attempt to choose vivid words or rhyming words	Vague and incorrect words
Sentences	Clear, correct sentences	Mostly clear, correct sentences	Many sentences clear and correct	Some sentences unclear or incorrect	Most sentences unclear or incorrect	Incoherent or incorrect sentences
Conventions	Excellent control; no capitalization errors	Good control; few capitalization errors	Fair control; some capitalization errors	Limited control; some capitalization errors affect meaning	Weak control; errors including capitalization affect clarity	Many serious errors prevent understanding

Rubric	5	4	3	2	1
Focus/Ideas	Strong focus on chosen topic; describes action	Clear focus on chosen topic; describes action	Unclear focus; some clear description	Weak focus on chosen topic; needs clearer description	Rambling lines on unclear topic; not a poem
Organization	Short poetic lines describe event in understandable sequence	Short poetic lines describe event in sequence	Some lines organized in sequence	Lines do not describe event in sequence	No recognizable sequence or arrangement
Voice	Imaginative and original	Mostly imaginative, original	Little imagination	Tries to be imaginative; not original	Not imaginative or original
Word Choice	Well-chosen, vivid words and rhyming words	Some well-chosen, vivid words and rhyming words	Weak language	Little attempt to choose vivid words or rhyming words	Vague and incorrect words
Sentences	Clear, correct sentences	Mostly clear, correct sentences	Some sentences unclear or incorrect	Most sentences unclear or incorrect	Incoherent or incorrect sentences
Conventions	Excellent control; no capitalization errors	Good control; few capitalization errors	Fair control; some capitalization errors	Weak control; errors including capitalization affect clarity	Many serious errors prevent understanding

Rubric	4	3	2	1
Focus/Ideas	Strong focus on chosen topic; describes action	Clear focus on chosen topic; describes action	Weak focus on chosen topic; needs clearer description	Rambling lines on unclear topic; not a poem
Organization	Short poetic lines describe event in understandable sequence	Short poetic lines describe event in sequence	Lines do not describe event in sequence	No recognizable sequence or arrangement
Voice	Imaginative and original	Mostly imaginative, original	Tries to be imaginative; not original	Not imaginative or original
Word Choice	Well-chosen, vivid words and rhyming words	Some well-chosen, vivid words and rhyming words	Little attempt to choose vivid words or rhyming words	Vague and incorrect words
Sentences	Clear, correct sentences	Mostly clear, correct sentences	Most sentences unclear or incorrect	Incoherent or incorrect sentences
Conventions	Excellent control; no capitalization errors	Good control; few capitalization errors	Weak control; errors including capitalization affect clarity	Many serious errors prevent understanding

Rubric	6	5	4	3	2	1
Focus/Ideas	Excellent, focused description of real things; strong, vivid details	Good focused description of real things; some vivid details	Description generally focused; few vivid details	Description not always focused; needs more vivid details	Weak focus; few vivid details	Description not focused; no vivid details
Organization	Topic identified early; details of appearance and action make sense	Topic identified early; details and order generally make sense	Topic not identified early; details and order unclear	Topic not identified early; details confused	Topic not identified early; details	Topic not clearly identified; no order to details
Voice	Clearly shows writer's mental pictures of chosen topic	Shows writer's mental images of chosen topic	Writer's mental image shown at times	Doesn't clearly show writer's mental images	Writer's feelings or interest not evident in description	Doesn't show writer's mental images or interest
Word Choice	Vivid, precise descriptive words paint a picture for readers	Many vivid, precise words help reader develop images	Some vivid, precise words	Few vivid, precise words	Vivid, precise words attempted	No vivid, precise words
Sentences	Complete, clear, and varied sentences	Complete, clear sentences; some variety	Few incomplete or unclear sentences	Some incomplete or unclear sentences	Several incomplete, unclear sentences	Incomplete, unclear sentences
Conventions	No mistakes or few mistakes; plural nouns correct	No serious mistakes; plural nouns correct	Few serious mistakes; few plural nouns incorrect	Some serious mistakes; some plural nouns incorrect	Many serious mistakes; many plural nouns incorrect	Numerous serious mistakes; plural nouns incorrect

Rubric	5	4	3	2	1
Focus/Ideas	Excellent, focused description of real things; strong, vivid details	Good focused description of real things; some vivid details	Description generally focused; few vivid details	Description not always focused; needs more vivid details	Description not focused; no vivid details
Organization	Topic identified early; details of appearance and action make sense	Topic identified early; details and order generally make sense	Topic not identified early; details and order unclear	Topic not identified early; details confused	Topic not clearly identified; no order to details
Voice	Clearly shows writer's mental pictures of chosen topic	Shows writer's mental images of chosen topic	Writer's mental image shown at times	Doesn't clearly show writer's mental images	Doesn't show writer's mental images or interest
Word Choice	Vivid, precise descriptive words paint a picture for readers	Many vivid, precise words help reader develop images	Some vivid, precise words	Few vivid, precise words	No vivid, precise words
Sentences	Complete, clear, and varied sentences	Complete, clear sentences; some variety	Few incomplete or unclear sentences	Some incomplete or unclear sentences	Incomplete, unclear sentences
Conventions	No mistakes or few mistakes; plural nouns correct	No serious mistakes; plural nouns correct	Few serious mistakes; few plural nouns incorrect	Some serious mistakes; some plural nouns incorrect	Many serious mistakes; plural nouns incorrect

Rubric	4	3	2	1
Focus/Ideas	Excellent, focused description of real things; strong, vivid details	Good focused description of real things; some vivid details	Description not always focused; needs more vivid details	Description not focused; no vivid details
Organization	Topic identified early; details of appearance and action make sense	Topic identified early; details and order generally make sense	Topic not identified early; details confused	Topic not clearly identified; no order to details
Voice	Clearly shows writer's mental pictures of chosen topic	Shows writer's mental images of chosen topic	Doesn't clearly show writer's mental images	Doesn't show writer's mental images or interest
Word Choice	Vivid, precise descriptive words paint a picture for readers	Some vivid, precise words help reader develop images	Few vivid, precise words	No vivid, precise words
Sentences	Complete, clear, and varied sentences	Complete, clear sentences; some variety	Some incomplete or unclear sentences	Incomplete, unclear sentences
Conventions	No mistakes or few mistakes; plural nouns correct	No serious mistakes; plural nouns correct	Some serious mistakes; some plural nouns incorrect	Many serious mistakes; plural nouns incorrect

Rubric	6	5	4	3	2	1
Focus/Ideas	Clearly explains important ideas about the chosen topic	Explains important ideas about the chosen topic	Some ideas explained about the chosen topic	Few ideas explained about the chosen topic	Expresses few ideas about the chosen topic	Ideas do not explain or describe real things
Organization	Presents ideas and details in a logical order	Presents ideas and details generally in logical order	Some ideas and details are not in logical order	Many ideas and details are not in logical order	Logical order attempted at times	Lacks structure and logical order
Voice	Shows writer's interest in and understanding of the topic	Shows writer's interest in and basic understanding of topic	Writer's interest in and basic understanding of topic generally clear	Writer's interest and understanding of topic sometimes unclear	Little sense of writer's interest or understanding of topic	Does not show writer's interest or understanding
Word Choice	Vivid, precise words clearly explain and describe	Some vivid, precise words explain and describe	Few vivid, precise words to explain or describe	Weak language used to describe and explain	Dull or unclear language	Vague and incorrect words
Sentences	Clear, complete sentences of different lengths	Mostly clear, complete sentences of different lengths	Few unclear or incomplete sentences	Some unclear or incomplete sentences	Many unclear or incomplete sentences	Confusing or incomplete sentences
Conventions	Nouns used correctly in all sentences; few errors	Nouns used correctly in most sentences; few errors	Nouns used correctly at times; some errors	Weak use of nouns; few errors affect understanding	Limited use of nouns; some errors under understanding	Weak use of nouns; many errors prevent understanding

Rubric	5	4	3	2	1
Focus/Ideas	Clearly explains important ideas about the chosen topic	Explains important ideas about the chosen topic	Some ideas expressed about the chosen topic	Expresses few ideas about the chosen topic	Ideas do not explain or describe real things
Organization	Presents ideas and details in a logical order	Presents ideas and details generally in logical order	Some ideas and details are not in logical order	Many ideas and details are not in logical order	Lacks structure and logical order
Voice	Shows writer's interest in and understanding of the topic	Shows writer's interest in and basic understanding of topic	Writer's interest and understanding of topic sometimes unclear	Little sense of writer's interest or understanding of topic	Does not show writer's interest or understanding
Word Choice	Vivid, precise words clearly explain and describe	Some vivid, precise words explain and describe	Few vivid, precise words to explain or describe	Weak language used to describe and explain	Vague and incorrect words
Sentences	Clear, complete sentences of different lengths	Mostly clear, complete sentences of different lengths	Few unclear or incomplete sentences	Some unclear or incomplete sentences	Confusing or incomplete sentences
Conventions	Nouns used correctly in all sentences; few errors	Nouns used correctly in most sentences; few errors	Nouns used correctly at times; some errors	Weak use of nouns; enough errors to hinder understanding	Weak use of nouns; many errors prevent understanding

Rubric	4	3	2	1
Focus/Ideas	Clearly explains important ideas about the chosen topic	Explains important ideas about the chosen topic	Expresses some ideas about the chosen topic	Ideas do not explain or describe real things
Organization	Presents ideas and details in a logical order	Presents ideas and details generally in logical order	Some ideas and details are not in logical order	Lacks structure and logical order
Voice	Shows writer's interest in and understanding of the topic	Shows writer's interest in and basic understanding of topic	Little sense of writer's interest or understanding of topic	Does not show writer's interest or understanding
Word Choice	Vivid, precise words clearly explain and describe	Some vivid, precise words explain and describe	Few vivid, precise words to explain or describe	Vague and incorrect words
Sentences	Clear, complete sentences of different lengths	Mostly clear, complete sentences of different lengths	Some unclear or incomplete sentences	Confusing or incomplete sentences
Conventions	Nouns used correctly in all sentences; few errors	Nouns used correctly in most sentences; few errors	Weak use of nouns; enough errors to hinder understanding	Weak use of nouns; many errors prevent understanding

Rubric	6	5	4	3	2	1
Focus/Ideas	Coherent story with characters, setting, and events that seem real	Story's characters, setting, and events seem real	Story's characters, setting, and events plausible	Characters, setting, or events plausible, but need more details	Not all of story's characters, setting, or events seem real	Characters, setting, or events unclear or unrealistic
Organization	Has well-developed beginning, middle, and end	Has beginning, middle, and end	Has beginning, middle, and end with few lapses	Sometimes unclear beginning, middle, or end, or events out of order	Unclear beginning, middle, or end, or events out of order	Order of events somewhat jumbled
Voice	Original story reflects writer's interest	Reflects writer's interest or involvement	Shows some of the writer's interest or involvement	Attempts to show writer's interest or involvement	Does not clearly reflect writer's interest or involvement	Little evidence of writer interest or involvement
Word Choice	Vivid action verbs and transition words bring story to life	Clear action verbs and transition words make story understandable	Some action verbs and transition words make story understandable	Fair use of action verbs and other words	Adequate action verbs and other words	Lacks clear action verbs, vivid words, and transition words
Sentences	All sentences clear and complete	Most sentences clear and complete	Sentences generally clear and complete	Sentences generally complete, some inconsistencies	Some unclear and incomplete sentences	Many unclear or incomplete sentences
Conventions	Few or no errors in spelling, verb use, other conventions	Errors in spelling or verb use do not hinder understanding	Some errors in spelling or verb use, does not generally hinder understanding	Occasional errors in spelling or verb use hinder understanding	Errors in spelling or verb use hinder understanding	Spelling and verb errors prevent understanding

Rubric	5	4	3	2	1
Focus/Ideas	Coherent story with characters, setting, and events that seem real	Story's characters, setting, and events seem real	Story's characters, setting, and events plausible	Not all of story's characters, setting, or events seem real	Characters, setting, or events unclear or unrealistic
Organization	Has well-developed beginning, middle, and end	Has beginning, middle, and end	Has beginning, middle, and end with few lapses	Unclear beginning, middle, or end, or events out of order	Order of events somewhat jumbled
Voice	Original story reflects writer's interest	Reflects writer's interest or involvement	Shows some of the writer's interest or involvement	Does not clearly reflect writer's interest or involvement	Little evidence of writer interest or involvement
Word Choice	Vivid action verbs and transition words bring story to life	Clear action verbs and transition words make story understandable	Some action verbs and transition words make story understandable	Adequate action verbs and other words	Lacks clear action verbs, vivid words, and transition words
Sentences	All sentences clear and complete	Most sentences clear and complete	Sentences generally clear and complete	Some unclear and incomplete sentences	Many unclear or incomplete sentences
Conventions	Few or no errors in spelling, verb use, other conventions	Errors in spelling or verb use do not hinder understanding	Some errors in spelling or verb use, does not generally hinder understanding	Errors in spelling or verb use hinder understanding	Spelling and verb errors prevent understanding

Rubric	4	3	2	1
Focus/Ideas	Coherent story with characters, setting, and events that seem real	Story's characters, setting, and events seem real	Not all of story's characters, setting, or events seem real	Characters, setting, or events unclear or unrealistic
Organization	Has well-developed beginning, middle, and end	Has beginning, middle, and end	Unclear beginning, middle, or end, or events out of order	Order of events somewhat jumbled
Voice	Original story reflects writer's interest	Reflects writer's interest or involvement	Does not clearly reflect writer's interest or involvement	Little evidence of writer interest or involvement
Word Choice	Vivid action verbs and transition words bring story to life	Clear action verbs and transition words make story understandable	Adequate action verbs and other words	Lacks clear action verbs, vivid words, and transition words
Sentences	All sentences clear and complete	Most sentences clear and complete	Some unclear and incomplete sentences	Many unclear or incomplete sentences
Conventions	Few or no errors in spelling, verb use, other conventions	Errors in spelling or verb use do not hinder understanding	Errors in spelling or verb use hinder understanding	Spelling and verb errors prevent understanding

Rubric	6	5	4	3	2	1
Focus/Ideas	Clearly focuses on two things Ruby does that the writer likes	Focuses on two things Ruby does that the writer likes	Adequate focus on two things Ruby does that the writer likes	Focus on at least one part of story; opinion clear at times	Weak focus on parts of story; opinion may be unclear	Not focused on story; opinion unclear
Organization	Identifies two actions by character and clear reasons for liking them	Identifies two actions by character and reasons for liking them	Identifies actions by character and reasons for liking them	Fair attempt to identify character's actions; may lack reasons	Attempts to identify character's actions; needs reasons	Statements not organized; reasons missing
Voice	Expresses writer's choices and feelings about the story	Expresses writer's choices and feelings about the story fairly well	Adequately expresses writer's choices and feelings about the story	Writer's choices and feelings about the story inconsistent	Writer's choices and feelings about the story not clear	Shows little interest or personal choice
Word Choice	Effective use of exact and vivid words	Good use of exact and vivid words	Uses exact and vivid words	Fair, albeit scattered, use of exact or vivid words	Uses a few exact or vivid words	Vague or incorrect words
Sentences	Clear and complete sentences for both parts of the story	Complete sentences for both parts of the story	Mostly complete sentences for both parts of the story	Inconsistent use of complete sentences	Sentences not complete or related to two parts of story	Incomplete or unclear sentences
Conventions	Correct use of verbs in sentences; correct spelling	Correct use of verbs in most sentences; few spelling errors	Correct use of verbs in most sentences; some errors	Fair use of verbs in some sentences; some spelling errors	Incorrect use of verbs in some sentences; too many spelling errors	Errors prevent understanding

Rubric	5	4	3	2	1
Focus/Ideas	Clearly focuses on two things Ruby does that the writer likes	Focuses on two things Ruby does that the writer likes	Adequate focus on two things Ruby does that the writer likes	Weak focus on two parts of story; opinion may be unclear	Not focused on story; opinion unclear
Organization	Identifies two actions by character and clear reasons for liking them	Identifies two actions by character and reasons for liking them	Identifies actions by character and reasons for liking them	Attempts to identify character's actions; needs reasons	Statements not organized; reasons missing
Voice	Expresses writer's choices and feelings about the story	Expresses writer's choices and feelings about the story fairly well	Adequately expresses writer's choices and feelings about the story	Writer's choices and feelings about the story not clear	Shows little interest or personal choice
Word Choice	Effective use of exact and vivid words	Good use of exact and vivid words	Fair use of exact and vivid words	Uses a few exact or vivid words	Vague or incorrect words
Sentences	Clear and complete sentences for both parts of the story	Complete sentences for both parts of the story	Mostly complete sentences for both parts of the story	Sentences not complete or related to two parts of story	Incomplete or unclear sentences
Conventions	Correct use of verbs in sentences; correct spelling	Correct use of verbs in most sentences; few spelling errors	Correct use of verbs in most sentences; some spelling errors	Incorrect use of verbs in some sentences; too many spelling errors	Errors prevent understanding

Rubric	4	3	2	1
Focus/Ideas	Clearly focuses on two things Ruby does that the writer likes	Focuses on two things Ruby does that the writer likes	Weak focus on two parts of story; opinion may be unclear	Not focused on story; opinion unclear
Organization	Identifies two actions by character and clear reasons for liking them	Identifies two actions by character and reasons for liking them	Attempts to identify character's actions; needs reasons	Statements not organized; reasons missing
Voice	Expresses writer's choices and feelings about the story	Expresses writer's choices and feelings about the story fairly well	Writer's choices and feelings about the story not clear	Shows little interest or personal choice
Word Choice	Effective use of exact and vivid words	Good use of exact and vivid words	Uses a few exact or vivid words	Vague or incorrect words
Sentences	Clear and complete sentences for both parts of the story	Complete sentences for both parts of the story	Sentences not complete or related to two parts of story	Incomplete or unclear sentences
Conventions	Correct use of verbs in sentences; correct spelling	Correct use of verbs in most sentences; few spelling errors	Incorrect use of verbs in some sentences; too many spelling errors	Errors prevent understanding

Rubric

Rubric	6	5	4	3	2	1
Focus/Ideas	Clearly tells the most important ideas and events of the selection	Tells important ideas and events of the selection	Tells fairly important ideas and events of the selection	Focus on selection ideas and events may be inconsistent	Not always focused on selection ideas and events	Not focused on selection ideas and events; not a summary
Organization	Expresses the ideas in the correct order	Expresses most ideas in the correct order	Generally expresses ideas in the correct order	Occasionally expresses ideas in different order than the selection	Expresses ideas in different order than the selection	Includes ideas in unclear or jumbled order
Voice	Reflects writer's good understanding of ideas in *The Class Pet*	Reflects writer's understanding of most ideas in *The Class Pet*	Reflects writer's understanding of some ideas in *The Class Pet*	Reflects understanding of some ideas in *The Class Pet*	Reflects understanding of some ideas in *The Class Pet*	Shows little understanding of ideas in *The Class Pet*
Word Choice	Excellent descriptive words and words that show time order	Good descriptive words and/or words that show time order	Fair use of descriptive words and/or words that show time order	Some descriptive words or words that show time order	Few descriptive words or words that show time order	No descriptive words or words that show time order
Sentences	All sentences are complete; sentences are varied	Most sentences are complete; some sentence variety	Sentences are fairly complete; some variety	Sentences may be incomplete; inconsistent variety	Sentences are incomplete; limited sentence variety	Sentences are incomplete, carelessly written, or unclear
Conventions	Uses correct verbs with singular and plural sentence subjects	Uses correct verbs with most singular and plural sentence subjects	Fair use of correct verbs with singular and plural sentence subjects	Occasionally uses incorrect verbs with singular and plural sentence subjects	Uses incorrect verbs with singular and plural sentence subjects	Incorrect verbs and other errors prevent understanding

Rubric

Rubric	5	4	3	2	1
Focus/Ideas	Clearly tells the most important ideas and events of the selection	Tells important ideas and events of the selection	Tells fairly important ideas and events of the selection	Not always focused on selection ideas and events	Not focused on selection ideas and events; not a summary
Organization	Expresses the ideas in the correct order	Expresses most ideas in the correct order	Generally expresses ideas in the correct order	Expresses ideas in different order than the selection	Includes ideas in unclear or jumbled order
Voice	Reflects writer's good understanding of ideas in *The Class Pet*	Reflects writer's understanding of most ideas in *The Class Pet*	Reflects writer's understanding of some ideas in *The Class Pet*	Reflects understanding of few ideas in *The Class Pet*	Shows little understanding of ideas in *The Class Pet*
Word Choice	Uses descriptive words and words that show time order	Uses some descriptive words and/or words that show time order	Fair use of descriptive words and/or words that show time order	Uses few descriptive words or words that show time order	No descriptive words or words that show time order
Sentences	All sentences are complete; sentences are varied	Most sentences are complete; some sentences varied	Sentences are fairly complete; some variety	Sentences are incomplete; limited sentence variety	Sentences are incomplete, carelessly written, or unclear
Conventions	Uses correct verbs with singular and plural sentence subjects	Uses correct verbs with most singular and plural sentence subjects	Fair use of correct verbs with singular and plural sentence subjects	Uses incorrect verbs with singular and plural sentence subjects	Incorrect verbs and other errors prevent understanding

Rubric

Rubric	4	3	2	1
Focus/Ideas	Clearly tells the most important ideas and events of the selection	Tells important ideas and events of the selection	Not always focused on selection ideas and events	Not focused on selection ideas and events; not a summary
Organization	Expresses the ideas in the correct order	Expresses most ideas in the correct order	Expresses ideas in different order than the selection	Includes ideas in unclear or jumbled order
Voice	Reflects writer's good understanding of ideas in *The Class Pet*	Reflects writer's understanding of most ideas in *The Class Pet*	Reflects understanding of some ideas in *The Class Pet*	Shows little understanding of ideas in *The Class Pet*
Word Choice	Uses descriptive words and words that show time order	Uses some descriptive words and/or words that show time order	Uses few descriptive words or words that show time order	No descriptive words or words that show time order
Sentences	All sentences are complete; sentences are varied	Most sentences are complete; some sentences variety	Sentences are incomplete; limited sentence variety	Sentences are incomplete, carelessly written, or unclear
Conventions	Uses correct verbs with singular and plural sentence subjects	Uses correct verbs with most singular and plural sentence subjects	Uses incorrect verbs with singular and plural sentence subjects	Incorrect verbs and other errors prevent understanding

Rubric	6	5	4	3	2	1
Focus/Ideas	Clear sentences telling Toad's actions that helped and didn't help	Sentences tell Toad's actions that helped and didn't help	Most sentences tell Toad's actions that helped and didn't help	Some sentences don't tell Toad's actions that helped or didn't help	Few sentences tell Toad's actions that helped or didn't help	Sentences lack focus on Toad's actions and whether they helped
Organization	Strong headings and sentences in format of two contrasting lists	Helpful headings and sentences form two lists	Headings and sentences adequate, form two lists	Some inconsistencies in headings and sentences	Missing one heading or one or two sentences; lists incomplete	Does not follow format of two lists with headings and sentences
Voice	Reflects writer's interest in and understanding of the topic	Reflects writer's interest in and some understanding of topic	Fair reflection of writer's interest and understanding of topic	Shows some understanding of or interest in topic, with some inconsistency	Does not show writer's interest or much understanding of topic	Uninvolved or indifferent writing
Word Choice	Uses clear and exact words to tell about character's actions	Some clear and exact words tell about character's actions	Fair use of clear and exact words that tell about character's actions	Some words tell about character's actions	Few clear or exact words to tell about character's actions	Words incorrect, unclear, or limited
Sentences	Headings and sentences clear and constructed correctly	Headings and most sentences clear and constructed correctly	Most headings and sentences constructed correctly	Some sentences or headings clear and constructed correctly	Few sentences or headings clear and constructed correctly	Sentences incomplete, incorrect, or unrelated
Conventions	Excellent control; few or no errors	Good control; no serious errors	Some control; minor errors do not affect understanding	Some errors affect reader's understanding	Weak control; errors affect reader's understanding	Many serious errors prevent understanding

Rubric	5	4	3	2	1
Focus/Ideas	Clear sentences telling Toad's actions that helped and didn't help	Sentences tell Toad's actions that helped and didn't help	Most sentences tell Toad's actions that helped and didn't help	Some sentences don't tell Toad's actions that helped or didn't help	Sentences lack focus on Toad's actions and whether they helped
Organization	Strong headings and sentences in format of two contrasting lists	Headings and sentences form two lists	Headings and sentences adequate, form two lists	Missing one heading or one or two sentences; lists incomplete	Does not follow format of two lists with headings and sentences
Voice	Reflects writer's interest in and understanding of the topic	Reflects writer's interest in and some understanding of topic	Fair reflection of writer's interest and understanding of topic	Does not show writer's interest or much understanding of topic	Uninvolved or indifferent writing
Word Choice	Uses clear and exact words to tell about character's actions	Some clear and exact words tell about character's actions	Fair use of clear and exact words that tell about character's actions	Few clear or exact words to tell about character's actions	Words incorrect, unclear, or limited
Sentences	Headings and sentences clear and constructed correctly	Headings and most sentences clear and constructed correctly	Headings and sentences constructed correctly	Few sentences or headings clear and constructed correctly	Sentences incomplete, incorrect, or unrelated
Conventions	Excellent control; few or no errors	Good control; no serious errors	Some control; minor errors do not affect understanding	Weak control; errors affect reader's understanding	Many serious errors prevent understanding

Rubric	4	3	2	1
Focus/Ideas	Clear sentences telling Toad's actions that helped and didn't help	Sentences tell Toad's actions that helped and didn't help	Some sentences don't tell Toad's actions that helped or didn't help	Sentences lack focus on Toad's actions and whether they helped
Organization	Strong headings and sentences in format of two contrasting lists	Headings and sentences form two lists	Missing one heading or one or two sentences; lists incomplete	Does not follow format of two lists with headings and sentences
Voice	Reflects writer's interest in and understanding of the topic	Reflects writer's interest in and some understanding of topic	Does not show writer's interest or much understanding of topic	Uninvolved or indifferent writing
Word Choice	Uses clear and exact words to tell about character's actions	Some clear and exact words tell about character's actions	Few clear or exact words to tell about character's actions	Words incorrect, unclear, or limited
Sentences	Headings and sentences clear and constructed correctly	Headings and most sentences clear and constructed correctly	Few sentences or headings clear and constructed correctly	Sentences incomplete, incorrect, or unrelated
Conventions	Excellent control; few or no errors	Good control; no serious errors	Weak control; errors affect reader's understanding	Many serious errors prevent understanding

Rubric	6	5	4	3	2	1
Focus/Ideas	Pictures show a change; captions clearly explain the pictures	Pictures show a change; captions explain pictures to a degree	Most pictures show a change; captions explain pictures to a degree	Captions show some attempt to explain the pictures	Captions show little attempt to explain the pictures	Captions do not explain pictures; topic is unclear
Organization	Two pictures reflect chosen topic; each has a pertinent caption	Two pictures reflect chosen topic; each has a caption	Two pictures fairly reflect chosen topic; each has a caption	Pictures relate to chosen topic; captions adequate	Pictures relate to chosen topic; captions not distinct	Ideas or images muddled or missing
Voice	Clearly reflects the purpose; captions show keen observation	Generally reflects the purpose; captions show observation	Adequately reflects the purpose; captions show some observation	Writing may not consistently reflect the purpose or careful observation	Writing doesn't clearly reflect the purpose or careful observation	Doesn't reflect the purpose or observation
Word Choice	Precise, vivid words relate to the images	Some precise or vivid words relate to the images	Fair use of precise or vivid words relate to the images	Some precise words about the images	Few precise or vivid words about the images	Vague or incorrect words
Sentences	Complete, clear sentences	Complete and fairly clear sentences	Generally complete and clear sentences	Occasionally unclear sentences	Some sentences incomplete or unclear	Sentences incomplete and unclear
Conventions	Excellent control; few or no errors	Good control; no serious errors	Fair control; no major errors	Inconsistent control; enough errors to affect understanding	Weak control; enough errors to affect understanding	Many serious errors prevent understanding

Rubric	5	4	3	2	1
Focus/Ideas	Pictures show a change; captions clearly explain the pictures	Pictures show a change; captions explain pictures to a degree	Most pictures show a change; captions explain pictures to a degree	Captions show an attempt to explain the pictures	Captions do not explain pictures; topic is unclear
Organization	Two pictures reflect chosen topic; each has a pertinent caption	Two pictures reflect chosen topic; each has a caption	Two pictures fairly reflect chosen topic; each has a caption	Pictures relate to chosen topic; captions not distinct	Ideas or images muddled or missing
Voice	Clearly reflects the purpose; captions show keen observation	Generally reflects the purpose; captions show observation	Adequately reflects the purpose; captions show some observation	Writing doesn't clearly reflect the purpose or careful observation	Doesn't reflect the purpose or observation
Word Choice	Precise, vivid words relate to the images	Some precise or vivid words relate to the images	Fair use of precise or vivid words relate to the images	Few precise or vivid words about the images	Vague or incorrect words
Sentences	Complete, clear sentences	Complete and fairly clear sentences	Generally complete and clear sentences	Some sentences incomplete or unclear	Sentences incomplete and unclear
Conventions	Excellent control; few or no errors	Good control; no serious errors	Fair control; no major errors	Weak control; enough errors to affect understanding	Many serious errors prevent understanding

Rubric	4	3	2	1
Focus/Ideas	Pictures show a change; captions clearly explain the pictures	Pictures show a change; captions explain pictures to a degree	Captions show an attempt to explain the pictures	Captions do not explain pictures; topic is unclear
Organization	Two pictures reflect chosen topic; each has a pertinent caption	Two pictures reflect chosen topic; each has a caption	Pictures relate to chosen topic; captions not distinct	Ideas or images muddled or missing
Voice	Clearly reflects the purpose; captions show keen observation	Generally reflects the purpose; captions show observation	Writing doesn't clearly reflect the purpose or careful observation	Doesn't reflect the purpose or observation
Word Choice	Precise, vivid words relate to the images	Some precise or vivid words relate to the images	Few precise or vivid words about the images	Vague or incorrect words
Sentences	Complete, clear sentences	Complete and fairly clear sentences	Some sentences incomplete or unclear	Sentences incomplete and unclear
Conventions	Excellent control; few or no errors	Good control; no serious errors	Weak control; enough errors to affect understanding	Many serious errors prevent understanding

Rubric	6	5	4	3	2	1
Focus/Ideas	Presents excellent dialogue between three characters from play	Presents good dialogue between three characters from play	Presents fair dialogue between three characters from play	Attempts adequate dialogue between characters from play	Attempts dialogue between characters from play	Dialogue does not reflect the characters; ideas unclear
Organization	Correctly follows format: character names followed by lines they say	Follows play format: character names and lines	Mostly follows play format: character names and lines	Play format inconsistent; characters or lines sometimes unclear	Play format not correct; characters or lines unclear	Does not follow play format; scene undeveloped
Voice	Shows knowledge of play and interest in new scene; original	Shows some knowledge of play and interest in new scene	Shows fair knowledge of play and interest in new scene	Shows some knowledge of play; scene is not original	Shows little knowledge of play; scene is not original	Shows little interest in play or new scene
Word Choice	Uses vivid and exact words in interesting ways	Uses some vivid and exact words	Fair use of vivid or exact words	Uses some vivid or exact words	Uses few vivid or exact words	Vague or incorrect words and character names
Sentences	Strong variety of clear, correct sentences	Variety of clear, correct sentences	Some variety of clear, correct sentences	Some sentences unclear, correct, or varied	Most sentences unclear, correct, or varied	Sentences not clear or complete
Conventions	Excellent control; few or no errors in spelling or conventions	Good control; no serious errors in spelling or conventions	Decent control; no serious errors in spelling or conventions	Average control; some errors affect understanding	Weak control; errors affect understanding	Serious errors prevent understanding

Rubric	5	4	3	2	1
Focus/Ideas	Presents excellent dialogue between three characters from play	Presents good dialogue between three characters from play	Presents fair dialogue between three characters from play	Attempts dialogue between characters from play	Dialogue does not reflect the characters; ideas unclear
Organization	Correctly follows format: character names followed by lines they say	Follows play format: character names and lines	Mostly follows play format: character names and lines	Play format not correct; characters or lines unclear	Does not follow play format; scene undeveloped
Voice	Shows knowledge of play and interest in new scene; original	Shows some knowledge of play and interest in new scene	Shows fair knowledge of play and interest in new scene	Shows little knowledge of play; scene is not original	Shows little interest in play or new scene
Word Choice	Uses vivid and exact words in interesting ways	Uses some vivid and exact words	Fair use of vivid or exact words	Uses few vivid or exact words	Vague or incorrect words and character names
Sentences	Strong variety of clear, correct sentences	Variety of clear, correct sentences	Some variety of clear, correct sentences	Sentences not very clear, correct, or varied	Sentences not clear or complete
Conventions	Excellent control; few or no errors in spelling or conventions	Good control; no serious errors in spelling or conventions	Decent control; no serious errors in spelling or conventions	Weak control; errors affect understanding	Serious errors prevent understanding

Rubric	4	3	2	1
Focus/Ideas	Presents excellent dialogue between three characters from play	Presents good dialogue between three characters from play	Attempts dialogue between characters from play	Dialogue does not reflect the characters; ideas unclear
Organization	Correctly follows format: character names followed by lines they say	Follows play format: character names and lines they say	Play format not correct; characters or lines unclear	Does not follow play format; scene undeveloped
Voice	Shows knowledge of play and interest in new scene; original	Shows some knowledge of play and interest in new scene	Shows little knowledge of play; scene is not original	Shows little interest in play or new scene
Word Choice	Uses vivid and exact words in interesting ways	Uses some vivid and exact words	Uses few vivid or exact words	Vague or incorrect words and character names
Sentences	Strong variety of clear, correct sentences	Variety of clear, correct sentences	Sentences not very clear, correct, or varied	Sentences not clear or complete
Conventions	Excellent control; few or no errors in spelling or conventions	Good control; no serious errors in spelling or conventions	Weak control; errors affect understanding	Serious errors prevent understanding

Rubric	6	5	4	3	2	1
Focus/Ideas	Interesting friendly letter with clear ideas about a surprise gift	Generally clear friendly letter with ideas about a surprise gift	Friendly letter generally focused; adequate ideas about a surprise gift	Friendly letter has some focus and ideas about a surprise gift	Friendly letter drifts from topic of a gift; ideas not always clear	Letter with no focus or development
Organization	Has greeting, sentences in sensible sequence, closing, and signature	Has greeting, sentences in understandable order, closing, and signature	Letter parts generally complete; mostly logical sequence	One or more letter parts missing; out-of-sequence at times	One or more letter parts missing; sentences not in logical sequence	Letter parts missing; sentences lack order
Voice	Strongly expresses writer's ideas and feelings in a friendly voice	Expresses writer's ideas and feelings in a friendly voice	Expresses writer's ideas and feelings adequately; friendly voice	Attempted expression of ideas and feelings, not very engaging	Limited expression of friendly voice or interest	No identifiable voice or ideas
Word Choice	Uses vivid, exact adjectives and other words to describe effectively	Most adjectives and other words to describe used effectively	Uses adjectives and other words to describe	Word choice adequate but lacks color	Limited word choice; few words that describe	Lacks words that describe
Sentences	Complete and varied sentences	Complete sentences; some variety	Sentences mostly clear	Some sentences unclear	Some incomplete or unclear sentences	Incomplete and unclear sentences
Conventions	No mistakes or few mistakes	No serious mistakes	Mistakes average, do not affect understanding	Mistakes may affect understanding	Numerous mistakes affect understanding	Mistakes detract from entire letter; hard to follow

Rubric	5	4	3	2	1
Focus/Ideas	Interesting friendly letter with clear ideas about a surprise gift	Generally clear friendly letter with ideas about a surprise gift	Friendly letter generally focused; adequate ideas about a surprise gift	Friendly letter drifts from topic of a gift; ideas not always clear	Letter lacks focus and idea about a surprise
Organization	Has greeting, sentences in sensible sequence, closing, and signature	Has greeting, sentences in understandable order, closing, and signature	Letter parts generally complete; mostly logical sequence	One or more letter parts missing; sentences not in sensible sequence	Letter parts missing; few sentences, in no apparent order
Voice	Strongly expresses writer's ideas and feelings in a friendly voice	Expresses writer's ideas and feelings in a friendly voice	Expresses writer's ideas and feelings adequately; friendly voice	Hardly expresses friendly voice or writer's interest	Lacks friendly voice and writer's interest
Word Choice	Uses vivid, exact adjectives and other words to describe effectively	Some adjectives and other words to describe used appropriately	Generally consistent word choice; some words that describe	Little word choice; few words that describe	Vague words; no words that describe
Sentences	Complete and varied sentences	Complete sentences; some variety	Generally clear sentences	Some incomplete or unclear sentences	Incomplete and unclear sentences
Conventions	No mistakes or few mistakes	No serious mistakes	Mistakes average, do not affect understanding	Many mistakes affect understanding	Too many mistakes; hard to understand

Rubric	4	3	2	1
Focus/Ideas	Interesting friendly letter with clear ideas about a surprise gift	Generally clear friendly letter with ideas about a surprise gift	Friendly letter drifts from topic of a gift; ideas not always clear	Letter lacks focus and idea about a surprise
Organization	Has greeting, sentences in sensible sequence, closing, and signature	Has greeting, sentences in understandable order, closing, and signature	One or more letter parts missing; sentences not in sensible sequence	Letter parts missing; few sentences, in no apparent order
Voice	Strongly expresses writer's ideas and feelings in a friendly voice	Expresses writer's ideas and feelings in a friendly voice	Hardly expresses friendly voice or writer's interest	Lacks friendly voice and writer's interest
Word Choice	Uses vivid, exact adjectives and other words to describe effectively	Some adjectives and other words to describe used effectively	Little word choice; few words that describe	Vague words; no words that describe
Sentences	Complete and varied sentences	Complete sentences; some variety	Some incomplete or unclear sentences	Incomplete and unclear sentences
Conventions	No mistakes or few mistakes	No serious mistakes	Many mistakes affect understanding	Too many mistakes; hard to understand

Rubric	6	5	4	3	2	1
Focus/Ideas	Invitation with strong focus on event, all relevant information	Invitation with clear focus on event, relevant information	Invitation with generally clear focus on event, relevant information	Invitation with adequate focus on event, some unclear information	Invitation not always focused on event or relevant details	Lacks focus on event or invitation; missing key information
Organization	All features of invitation in clear, logical order	Most features of invitation; clear order	Most features of invitation; fairly clear order	Most features of invitation; order not entirely consistent	Few features of invitation; order is not clear	Features of invitation not apparent; no meaningful order
Voice	Strongly aware of purpose; polite and informative	Aware of purpose; polite and generally informative	Aware of purpose; mostly polite and informative	Somewhat aware of purpose and audience	Uncertain of purpose; vague, lacking politeness or interest	Little indication of purpose, politeness, or interest
Word Choice	Clear, polite, and descriptive words; adjectives for colors and shapes	Most words clear, polite, or descriptive; adjectives for color or shape	Some words polite or descriptive; some adjectives for color or shape	Words occasionally polite or descriptive; few adjectives for color or shape	Few clear, polite, or descriptive words; needs adjectives	Vague or incorrect words
Sentences	All sentences correctly constructed; clear	Most sentences correctly constructed; clear	Some sentences correctly constructed; clear	Some sentences incorrectly constructed or unclear	Few sentences correctly constructed or clear	Sentences incorrect or incomplete
Conventions	Excellent control; dates correctly written; few or no errors	Good control; dates correctly written; no serious errors	Shows control; dates correctly written; errors minor	Some control, errors typically do not affect understanding	Weak control; enough errors to affect understanding	Many serious errors that prevent understanding

Rubric	5	4	3	2	1
Focus/Ideas	Invitation with strong focus on event, all relevant information	Invitation with clear focus on event, most relevant information	Invitation generally focused on event or relevant details	Invitation not always focused on event or relevant details	Lacks focus on event or invitation; missing key information
Organization	All features of invitation in clear, logical order	Most features of invitation; clear order	Some features of invitation; order generally clear	Few features of invitation; order is not clear	Features of invitation not apparent; no meaningful order
Voice	Strongly aware of purpose; polite and informative	Aware of purpose; polite and generally informative	Generally aware of purpose; informative	Uncertain of purpose; vague, lacking politeness or interest	Little indication of purpose, politeness, or interest
Word Choice	Clear, polite, and descriptive words; adjectives for colors and shapes	Most words clear, polite, or descriptive; adjectives for color or shape	Some words clear, polite, or descriptive; some adjectives for color or shape	Few clear, polite, or descriptive words; needs adjectives	Vague or incorrect words
Sentences	All sentences correctly constructed	Most sentences correctly constructed	Some sentences correctly constructed	Few sentences correctly constructed	Sentences incorrect or incomplete
Conventions	Excellent control; dates correctly written; few or no errors	Good control; dates correctly written; no serious errors	Some control, errors typically do not affect understanding	Weak control; enough errors to affect understanding	Many serious errors that prevent understanding

Rubric	4	3	2	1
Focus/Ideas	Invitation with strong focus on event, all relevant information	Invitation with clear focus on event, most relevant information	Invitation not always focused on event or relevant details	Lacks focus on event or invitation; missing key information
Organization	All features of invitation in clear, logical order	Most features of invitation; clear order	Few features of invitation; order is not clear	Features of invitation not apparent; no meaningful order
Voice	Strongly aware of purpose; polite and informative	Aware of purpose; polite and generally informative	Uncertain of purpose; vague, lacking politeness or interest	Little indication of purpose, politeness, or interest
Word Choice	Clear, polite, and descriptive words; adjectives for colors and shapes	Most words clear, polite, or descriptive; adjectives for color or shape	Few clear, polite, or descriptive words; needs adjectives	Vague or incorrect words
Sentences	All sentences correctly constructed	Most sentences correctly constructed	Few sentences correctly constructed	Sentences incorrect or incomplete
Conventions	Excellent control; dates correctly written; few or no errors	Good control; dates correctly written; no serious errors	Weak control; enough errors to affect understanding	Many serious errors that prevent understanding

DESCRIPTIVE POEM

Rubric	6	5	4	3	2	1
Focus/Ideas	Poem with strong, clear focus on describing a chosen place	Poem with clear focus on describing a chosen place	Poem with fairly clear focus on describing a chosen place	Poem with adequate focus on describing a chosen place	Poem with weak focus on a place; description unclear	Rambling lines; no clear description of topic; not a poem
Organization	Carefully organized in lines; images in sensible order	Organized in lines; images in sensible order	Reasonable organization of lines; images mostly in sensible order	Some organization of lines; images mostly in sensible order	Not consistently arranged in lines; images not in sensible order	No recognizable arrangement; images hard to distinguish
Voice	Creates mental picture; imaginative and original	Creates mental picture; mostly imaginative and original	Creates adequate mental picture; fairly imaginative and original	Attempts a mental picture; some originality	Attempts a mental picture; not very imaginative or original	No evidence of mental picture; not imaginative or original
Word Choice	Vivid words including adjectives about size; rhyming words	Some vivid words including adjectives for size; rhyming words	Generally vivid words, including adjectives for size; rhyming words	Vivid adjectives or other words used sparingly; some rhymes	Few vivid adjectives or other vivid words; incorrect rhymes	No vivid adjectives; vague or incorrect words
Sentences	Clear, correct sentences with variety	Mostly clear, correct sentences with some variety	Generally clear, correct sentences with some variety	Inconsistent sentences; variety	Most sentences unclear or incorrect; not much variety	Most sentences incoherent or incorrect
Conventions	Excellent control; uses adjectives well; few or no errors	Good control; uses adjectives; few or no serious errors	Generally good control; uses adjectives; some errors	Fair control; some serious errors	Weak control; few adjectives; errors affect understanding	Many serious errors prevent understanding

Rubric	5	4	3	2	1
Focus/Ideas	Poem with strong, clear focus on describing a chosen place	Poem with clear focus on describing a chosen place	Poem with fairly clear focus on describing a chosen place	Poem with weak focus on a place; description unclear	Rambling lines; no clear description of topic; not a poem
Organization	Carefully organized in lines; images in sensible order	Organized in lines; images mostly in sensible order	Reasonable organization of lines; images mostly in sensible order	Not consistently arranged in lines; images not in sensible order	No recognizable arrangement; images hard to distinguish
Voice	Creates mental picture; imaginative and original	Creates mental picture; mostly imaginative and original	Creates adequate mental picture; fairly imaginative and original	Attempts a mental picture; not very imaginative or original	No evidence of mental picture; not imaginative or original
Word Choice	Vivid words including adjectives about size; rhyming words	Some vivid words including adjectives for size; rhyming words	Generally vivid words, including adjectives for size; rhyming words	Few vivid adjectives or other vivid words; incorrect rhymes	No vivid adjectives; vague or incorrect words
Sentences	Clear, correct sentences with variety	Mostly clear, correct sentences with some variety	Generally clear, correct sentences with some variety	Most sentences unclear or incorrect; not much variety	Most sentences incoherent or incorrect
Conventions	Excellent control; uses adjectives well; few or no errors	Good control; uses adjectives; few or no serious errors	Generally good control; uses adjectives; some errors	Weak control; few adjectives; errors affect understanding	Many serious errors prevent understanding

Rubric	4	3	2	1
Focus/Ideas	Poem with strong, clear focus on describing a chosen place	Poem with clear focus on describing a chosen place	Poem with weak focus on a place; description unclear	Rambling lines; no clear description of topic; not a poem
Organization	Carefully organized in lines; images in sensible order	Organized in lines; images mostly in sensible order	Not consistently arranged in lines; images not in sensible order	No recognizable arrangement; images hard to distinguish
Voice	Creates mental picture; imaginative and original	Creates mental picture; mostly imaginative and original	Attempts a mental picture; not very imaginative or original	No evidence of mental picture; not imaginative or original
Word Choice	Vivid words including adjectives about size; rhyming words	Some vivid words including adjectives for size; rhyming words	Few vivid adjectives or other vivid words; incorrect rhymes	No vivid adjectives; vague or incorrect words
Sentences	Clear, correct sentences with variety	Mostly clear, correct sentences with some variety	Most sentences unclear or incorrect; not much variety	Most sentences incoherent or incorrect
Conventions	Excellent control; uses adjectives well; few or no errors	Good control; uses adjectives; few or no serious errors	Weak control; few adjectives; errors affect understanding	Many serious errors prevent understanding

Rubric	6	5	4	3	2	1
Focus/Ideas	Focused, realistic narrative that clearly tells characters' actions	Focused narrative that tells characters' actions	Generally focused narrative tells characters' actions	Narrative not always focused on characters' actions; not always realistic	Narrative not clearly focused on characters' actions; not realistic	Narrative not focused, developed, or realistic
Organization	Has well-developed beginning, middle, and end	Has beginning, middle, and end	Has adequate beginning, middle, and end	Order of events somewhat inconsistent	Events told in unclear order	Indistinct events in no reasonable order
Voice	Shows the writer's and characters' feelings and writer's interest	Shows characters' feelings; some interest on writer's part	Shows most characters' feelings; some interest on writer's part	Characters' feelings not entirely clear; limited interest on writer's part	Little evidence of characters' feelings or interest on writer's part	No evidence of characters' feelings or writer's interest
Word Choice	Vivid adjectives and other words describe characters, setting, and events	Several vivid adjectives describe characters, setting, and events	Some vivid adjectives describe characters, setting, and events	Limited descriptive words	Limited descriptive words; redundant language	Vague or misused words
Sentences	Varied sentences all clear and complete	Most sentences clear and complete; some variety	Sentences generally clear and complete; some variety	Few sentences clear and complete; limited variety	Few sentences clear and complete; not much variety	Many incomplete or incoherent sentences
Conventions	Uses adjectives for what kind correctly; few or no errors	Uses most adjectives correctly; few or no serious errors	Generally uses adjectives correctly; some errors	Fair use of adjectives; some errors that affect understanding	Uses adjectives incorrectly; errors affect understanding	Serious errors prevent understanding

Rubric	5	4	3	2	1
Focus/Ideas	Focused, realistic narrative that clearly tells characters' actions	Focused narrative that tells characters' actions	Generally focused narrative tells characters' actions	Narrative not clearly focused on characters' actions; not realistic	Narrative not focused, developed, or realistic
Organization	Has well-developed beginning, middle, and end	Has beginning, middle, and end	Has adequate beginning, middle, and end	Events told in unclear order	Indistinct events in no reasonable order
Voice	Shows the writer's and characters' feelings and writer's interest	Shows characters' feelings; some interest on writer's part	Shows most characters' feelings; some interest on writer's part	Little evidence of characters' feelings or interest on writer's part	No evidence of characters' feelings or writer's interest
Word Choice	Vivid adjectives and other words describe characters, setting, and events	Some vivid adjectives describe characters, setting, and events	Some vivid adjectives describe characters, setting, and events	Limited descriptive words; redundant language	Vague or misused words
Sentences	Varied sentences all clear and complete	Most sentences clear and complete; some variety	Sentences generally clear and complete; some variety	Few sentences clear and complete; not much variety	Many incomplete or incoherent sentences
Conventions	Uses adjectives for what kind correctly; few or no errors	Uses most adjectives correctly; few or no serious errors	Generally uses adjectives correctly; some errors	Uses adjectives incorrectly; errors affect understanding	Serious errors prevent understanding

Rubric	4	3	2	1
Focus/Ideas	Focused, realistic narrative that clearly tells characters' actions	Focused narrative that tells characters' actions	Narrative not clearly focused on characters' actions; not realistic	Narrative not focused, developed, or realistic
Organization	Has well-developed beginning, middle, and end	Has beginning, middle, and end	Events told in unclear order	Indistinct events in no reasonable order
Voice	Shows the writer's and characters' feelings and writer's interest	Shows characters' feelings; some interest on writer's part	Little evidence of characters' feelings or interest on writer's part	No evidence of characters' feelings or writer's interest
Word Choice	Vivid adjectives and other words describe characters, setting, and events	Some vivid adjectives describe characters, setting, and events	Limited descriptive words; redundant language	Vague or misused words
Sentences	Varied sentences all clear and complete	Most sentences clear and complete; some variety	Few sentences clear and complete; not much variety	Many incomplete or incoherent sentences
Conventions	Uses adjectives for what kind correctly; few or no errors	Uses most adjectives correctly; few or no serious errors	Uses adjectives incorrectly; errors affect understanding	Serious errors prevent understanding

Rubric	6	5	4	3	2	1
Focus/Ideas	Strong note clearly expresses thanks, identifying reason for thanks	Note clearly expresses thanks, identifying reason for thanks	Note expresses thanks, identifying reason for thanks	Some expression of thanks, reason for thanks	Shows some attempt to express thanks and the reason for thanks	Fails to express thanks or identify the reason for thanks
Organization	Strong control of letter format: date, greeting with comma, body, closing with comma	Appropriate letter format: date, greeting with comma, body, and closing with comma	Letter format correct: date, greeting, body, closing	Letter format generally correct: date, greeting, body, closing with minor errors	Letter format incorrect; errors in date, greeting, or closing	Missing more than two letter parts; not a thank-you note
Voice	Engaging, friendly voice	Mostly engaging, friendly voice	Fairly engaging, friendly voice	Somewhat engaging, friendly voice	Voice not engaging or not suitable to thank-you note	Not engaging, lacking friendly voice
Word Choice	Clear words of thanks, letter words, and number words as needed	Mostly clear words of thanks, letter words, and number words as needed	Uses words of thanks, letter words, and number words	Inconsistent use of words that show thanks, letter words, and number words	Missing or unclear words of thanks or letter words (such as *Dear*)	No words of thanks or letter words; vague or misused words
Sentences	All sentences clear, complete, and correct	Mostly clear, complete, and correct sentences	Most sentences clear, complete, and correct	Some sentences unclear, incomplete, or incorrect	Few sentences clear, complete, and correct	Most sentences unclear, incomplete, and incorrect
Conventions	Correct capitalization, punctuation, spelling, and number words	Mostly correct capitalization, punctuation, spelling, and number words	Few capitalization, punctuation, spelling, or number word errors	Several capitalization, punctuation, spelling, or number word errors	Multiple errors in language conventions affect understanding	Serious errors in language conventions prevent understanding

Rubric	5	4	3	2	1
Focus/Ideas	Strong note clearly expresses thanks, identifying reason for thanks	Note clearly expresses thanks, identifying reason for thanks	Note expresses thanks, identifying reason for thanks	Shows some attempt to express thanks and the reason for thanks	Fails to express thanks or identify the reason for thanks
Organization	Letter format: date, greeting with comma, body, closing with comma	Appropriate letter format: date, greeting with comma, body, and closing with comma	Letter format generally correct: date, greeting, body, closing	Letter format incorrect; errors in date, greeting, or closing	Missing more than two letter parts; not a thank-you note
Voice	Engaging, friendly voice	Mostly engaging, friendly voice	Fairly engaging, friendly voice	Voice not engaging or not suitable to thank-you note	Not engaging, lacking friendly voice
Word Choice	Clear words of thanks, letter words, and number words as needed	Mostly clear words of thanks, letter words, and number words as needed	Uses words of thanks, letter words, and number words	Missing or unclear words of thanks or letter words (such as *Dear*)	No words of thanks or letter words; vague or misused words
Sentences	All sentences clear, complete, and correct	Mostly clear, complete, and correct sentences	Most sentences clear, complete, and correct	Few sentences clear, complete, and correct	Most sentences unclear, incomplete, and incorrect
Conventions	Correct capitalization, punctuation, spelling, and number words	Mostly correct capitalization, punctuation, spelling, and number words	Few capitalization, punctuation, spelling, or number word errors	Multiple errors in language conventions affect understanding	Serious errors in language conventions prevent understanding

Rubric	4	3	2	1
Focus/Ideas	Strong note clearly expresses thanks, identifying reason for thanks	Note expresses thanks, identifying reason for thanks	Attempts to express thanks and the reason for thanks	Fails to express thanks or identify the reason for thanks
Organization	Letter format: date, greeting with comma, body, closing with comma	Letter format generally correct: date, greeting, body, closing	Letter format incorrect; errors in date, greeting, or closing	Missing more than two letter parts; not a thank-you note
Voice	Engaging, friendly voice	Mostly engaging, friendly voice	Voice not engaging or not suitable to thank-you note	Not engaging, lacking friendly voice
Word Choice	Clear words of thanks, letter words, and number words as needed	Uses words of thanks, letter words, and number words	Missing or unclear words of thanks or letter words (such as *Dear*)	No words of thanks or letter words; vague or misused words
Sentences	All sentences clear, complete, and correct	Most sentences clear, complete, and correct	Few sentences clear, complete, and correct	Most sentences unclear, incomplete, and incorrect
Conventions	Correct capitalization, punctuation, spelling, and number words	Few capitalization, punctuation, spelling, or number word errors	Multiple errors in language conventions affect understanding	Serious errors in language conventions prevent understanding

Rubric	6	5	4	3	2	1
Focus/Ideas	Clear directions; strong focus on gift making or activity planning	Mostly clear directions; good focus on gift making or activity	Fairly clear directions; adequate focus on gift making or activity	Directions generally focused, minor inconsistencies	Directions sometimes not focused on the topic	No real focus on topic; not written to direct the reader
Organization	All steps explained in proper, easy-to-understand order	Steps explained in proper, easy-to-understand order	Steps generally explained in proper, easy-to-understand order	Steps in order, some vague	Some steps missing or not in proper, understandable order	Not in understandable order; no sequence of steps
Voice	Clearly informed about the topic; enthusiastically expressed	Informed about the topic; for the most part, enthusiastic	Fairly informed about the topic; for the most part, enthusiastic	Attempts to be involved with the topic; wavering enthusiasm	Vaguely involved with the topic; not very enthusiastic	No evidence of involvement with topic
Word Choice	Uses clear verbs, adjectives, and words such as *first, next,* and *then*	Mostly clear verbs, adjectives, and words such as *first, next,* and *then*	Some clear verbs, adjectives, and words such as *first, next,* and *then*	Inconsistent use of clear verbs, adjectives, or words such as *first, next,* and *then*	Few clear verbs, adjectives, or words such as *first, next,* and *then*	Limited word choice; vague or incorrect adjectives and verbs
Sentences	Clear sentences, telling how something is done	Mostly clear sentences telling what should be done	Sentences tell what should be done	Some sentences unclear or incorrect	Many sentences unclear or incorrect	Incoherent and incorrect sentences
Conventions	Excellent control; few or no errors, including adjectives	Good control; no serious errors, including adjectives	Adequate control; errors minor	Fair control; several errors	Weak control; enough errors to affect understanding	Many serious errors that prevent understanding

Rubric	5	4	3	2	1
Focus/Ideas	Clear directions; strong focus on gift making or activity planning	Mostly clear directions; good focus on gift making or activity	Fairly clear directions; adequate focus on gift making or activity	Directions sometimes not focused on the topic	No real focus on topic; not written to direct the reader
Organization	All steps explained in proper, easy-to-understand order	Most steps explained in proper, easy-to-understand order	Steps generally explained in proper, easy-to-understand order	Some steps missing or not in proper, understandable order	Not in understandable order; no sequence of steps
Voice	Informed about the topic; enthusiastically expressed	Fairly informed about the topic; for the most part, enthusiastic	Fairly informed about the topic; for the most part, enthusiastic	Vaguely involved with the topic; not very enthusiastic	No evidence of involvement with topic
Word Choice	Uses clear verbs, adjectives, and words such as *first, next,* and *then*	Some clear verbs, adjectives, and words such as *first, next,* and *then*	Some clear verbs, adjectives, and words such as *first, next,* and *then*	Few clear verbs, adjectives, or words such as *first, next,* and *then*	Limited word choice; vague or incorrect adjectives and verbs
Sentences	Clear sentences, telling how something is done	Mostly clear sentences telling what should be done	Sentences tell what should be done	Many sentences unclear or incorrect	Incoherent and incorrect sentences
Conventions	Excellent control; few or no errors, including adjectives	Good control; no serious errors, including adjectives	Adequate control; errors minor	Weak control; enough errors to affect understanding	Many serious errors that prevent understanding

Rubric	4	3	2	1
Focus/Ideas	Clear directions; strong focus on gift making or activity planning	Mostly clear directions; good focus on gift making or activity	Directions sometimes not focused on the topic	No real focus on topic; not written to direct the reader
Organization	All steps explained in proper, easy-to-understand order	Most steps explained in proper, easy-to-understand order	Some steps missing or not in proper, understandable order	Not in understandable order; no sequence of steps
Voice	Informed about the topic; enthusiastically expressed	Fairly informed about the topic; for the most part, enthusiastic	Vaguely involved with the topic; not very enthusiastic	No evidence of involvement with topic
Word Choice	Uses clear verbs, adjectives, and words such as *first, next,* and *then*	Some clear verbs, adjectives, and words such as *first, next,* and *then*	Few clear verbs, adjectives, or words such as *first, next,* and *then*	Limited word choice; vague or incorrect adjectives and verbs
Sentences	Clear sentences, telling how something is done	Mostly clear sentences telling what should be done	Many sentences unclear or incorrect	Incoherent and incorrect sentences
Conventions	Excellent control; few or no errors, including adjectives	Good control; no serious errors, including adjectives	Weak control; enough errors to affect understanding	Many serious errors that prevent understanding

Rubric	6	5	4	3	2	1
Focus/Ideas	Animal story focused on topic; clear fantasy element and descriptive details	Animal story mostly focused on topic; fantasy element; clear details	Animal story at times focused on topic; fantasy element; few details	Animal story on topic at times; fantasy element generally clear	Animal story not always focused on topic; fantasy element unclear	Rambling narrative; lacks fantasy element; characters unclear
Organization	Story has identifiable problem that characters solve	Story has a problem that characters solve	Characters interact with problem, but do not solve it	Story includes clear problem	Attempts to include problem that characters solve	No identifiable story problem for characters to solve
Voice	Shows writer's engaging interest in characters and story events	Shows writer's interest in characters and events	Writer's interest evident	Writer's interest in characters evident at times	Needs to show more interest in characters and events	Does not show interest in characters and events
Word Choice	Vivid, precise words that bring the story to life	Language begins to give story life	Some vivid, precise words	Adequate language	Language adequate but lacks vitality	Vague or misused words
Sentences	All sentences clear and complete; uses imperative sentences	Most sentences clear and complete; an imperative sentence	Some sentences clear and complete; an imperative sentence	Some run-on or incomplete sentences; unclear imperative sentence	Many run-on or incomplete sentences; unclear imperative sentence	Many run-on or incomplete sentences; no imperative sentence
Conventions	Few or no errors, including imperative sentence structure	No serious errors; correct imperative sentence	Few serious errors; correct imperative sentence	Some errors; incorrect imperative sentence	Several errors; incorrect imperative sentence	Many errors that prevent understanding

Rubric	5	4	3	2	1
Focus/Ideas	Animal story focused on topic; fantasy element and clear details	Animal story mostly focused on topic; fantasy element; some detail	Animal story on topic at times; fantasy element apparent; lacking detail	Animal story not always focused on topic; fantasy element unclear	Rambling narrative; lacks fantasy element; characters unclear
Organization	Story has identifiable problem that characters solve	Story has a problem that characters solve	Story includes problem, but characters do not solve it	Attempts to include problem that characters solve	No identifiable story problem for characters to solve
Voice	Shows writer's engaging interest in characters and story events	Shows writer's interest in characters and events	Writer's interest in characters evident at times	Needs to show more interest in characters and events	Does not show interest in characters and events
Word Choice	Vivid, precise words that bring the story to life	Some vivid, precise words to give the story life	Adequate language	Language adequate but lacks vitality	Vague or misused words
Sentences	All sentences clear and complete; uses imperative sentences	Most sentences clear and complete; an imperative sentence	Some run-on or incomplete sentences; unclear imperative sentence	Many run-on or incomplete sentences; unclear imperative sentence	Many run-on or incomplete sentences; no imperative sentence
Conventions	Few or no errors, including imperative sentence structure	No serious errors; correct imperative sentence	Few errors; incorrect imperative sentence	Several errors; incorrect imperative sentence	Many errors that prevent understanding

Rubric	4	3	2	1
Focus/Ideas	Animal story focused on topic; fantasy element and clear details	Animal story mostly focused on topic; fantasy element; some detail	Animal story not always focused on topic; fantasy element unclear	Rambling narrative; lacks fantasy element; characters unclear
Organization	Story has identifiable problem that characters solve	Story has a problem that characters solve	Attempts to include problem that characters solve	No identifiable story problem for characters to solve
Voice	Shows writer's engaging interest in characters and story events	Shows writer's interest in characters and events	Needs to show more interest in characters and events	Does not show interest in characters and events
Word Choice	Vivid, precise words that bring the story to life	Some vivid, precise words to give the story life	Language adequate but lacks vitality	Vague or misused words
Sentences	All sentences clear and complete; uses imperative sentences	Most sentences clear and complete; an imperative sentence	Some run-on or incomplete sentences; unclear imperative sentence	Many run-on or incomplete sentences; no imperative sentence
Conventions	Few or no errors, including imperative sentence structure	No serious errors; correct imperative sentence	Several errors; incorrect imperative sentence	Many errors that prevent understanding

Rubric	6	5	4	3	2	1
Focus/Ideas	Addressed to Mole; clearly expresses writer's feelings on topic	Addressed to Mole; writer's feelings expressed well	Addressed to Mole; expresses writer's feelings on topic fairly well	Addressed to Mole; writer's feelings on topic expressed at times	Addressed to Mole; attempts to express writer's feelings on topic	Does not express writer's feelings on topic; not addressed to Mole
Organization	Friendly greeting and closing; story information and writer's ideas	All letter parts, story information, and writer's ideas included	Includes parts of letter and writer's ideas	Missing one letter part; ideas in fairly sensible order	Missing one or two letter parts; ideas not in sensible order	More than two letter parts missing; ideas not arranged
Voice	Shows clear knowledge of story and strongly states writer's feelings	Shows knowledge of story and writer's feelings stated	Shows some knowledge of story and states writer's feelings	Writer's feelings stated vaguely	Shows little knowledge of story; does not clearly state feelings	Lacks knowledge of story; uninvolved with topic
Word Choice	Vivid, precise words convey ideas and feelings; includes pronouns	Good use of vivid and precise words; includes pronouns	Many vivid, precise words for ideas and feelings; includes pronouns	Some vivid, precise words for ideas and feelings; includes some pronouns	Few vivid or precise words for ideas and feelings or pronouns	Vague or repeated words; no correct pronouns
Sentences	All sentences clear and complete; sentences are varied	Most sentences clear and complete; good sentence variety	Many sentences clear and complete; some sentence variety	Some sentences clear and complete; little sentence variety	Few sentences clear and complete; no sentence variety	Sentences unclear, incomplete, and unvaried
Conventions	Uses pronouns correctly; few or no language convention errors	Uses pronouns correctly; no serious errors with conventions	Uses pronouns correctly; few serious errors with conventions	Uses some pronouns correctly; a few serious errors with conventions	Uses pronouns incorrectly; serious errors with conventions	Many serious errors prevent understanding

Rubric	5	4	3	2	1
Focus/Ideas	Addressed to Mole; clearly expresses writer's feelings on topic	Addressed to Mole; expresses writer's feelings on topic fairly well	Addressed to Mole; writer's feelings on topic expressed at times	Addressed to Mole; attempts to express writer's feelings on topic	Does not express writer's feelings on topic; not addressed to Mole
Organization	Friendly greeting and closing; story information and writer's ideas	Includes parts of letter, story information, and writer's ideas	Missing one letter part; ideas in fairly sensible order	Missing one or two letter parts; ideas not in sensible order	More than two letter parts missing; ideas not arranged
Voice	Shows knowledge of story and strongly states writer's feelings	Shows some knowledge of story and states writer's feelings	Writer's feelings stated vaguely	Shows little knowledge of story; does not clearly state feelings	Lacks knowledge of story; uninvolved with topic
Word Choice	Vivid, precise words convey ideas and feelings; includes pronouns	Many vivid, precise words for ideas and feelings; includes pronouns	Some vivid, precise words for ideas and feelings; includes some pronouns	Few vivid or precise words for ideas and feelings or pronouns	Vague or repeated words; no correct pronouns
Sentences	All sentences clear and complete; sentences are varied	Most sentences clear and complete; good sentence variety	Some sentences clear and complete; some sentence variety	Few sentences clear and complete; little sentence variety	Sentences unclear, incomplete, and unvaried
Conventions	Uses pronouns correctly; few or no language convention errors	Uses pronouns correctly; no serious errors with conventions	Uses some pronouns correctly; a few serious errors with conventions	Uses pronouns incorrectly; serious errors with conventions	Many serious errors prevent understanding

Rubric	4	3	2	1
Focus/Ideas	Addressed to Mole; clearly expresses writer's feelings on topic	Addressed to Mole; expresses writer's feelings on topic fairly well	Addressed to Mole; attempts to express writer's feelings on topic	Does not express writer's feelings on topic; not addressed to Mole
Organization	Friendly greeting and closing; story information and writer's ideas	Includes parts of letter, story information, and writer's ideas	Missing one or two letter parts; ideas not in sensible order	More than two letter parts missing; ideas not arranged
Voice	Shows knowledge of story and strongly states writer's feelings	Shows some knowledge of story and states writer's feelings	Shows little knowledge of story; does not clearly state feelings	Lacks knowledge of story; uninvolved with topic
Word Choice	Vivid, precise words convey ideas and feelings; includes pronouns	Some vivid, precise words for ideas and feelings; includes pronouns	Few vivid or precise words for ideas and feelings or pronouns	Vague or repeated words; no correct pronouns
Sentences	All sentences clear and complete; sentences are varied	Most sentences clear and complete; some sentence variety	Few sentences clear and complete; little sentence variety	Sentences unclear, incomplete, and unvaried
Conventions	Uses pronouns correctly; few or no language convention errors	Uses pronouns correctly; no serious errors with conventions	Uses pronouns incorrectly; serious errors with conventions	Many serious errors prevent understanding

Rubric	6	5	4	3	2	1
Focus/Ideas	Three clear questions of interest to writer and a good answer to one	Three generally clear questions and a pertinent answer to one	Three questions; answer to one question unclear	Three questions but not all clear; attempts to answer one question	One or two sentences formed as questions; answer attempted, but unclear	Rambling sentences, not formed as questions; no clear answer
Organization	Asks three questions distinctly, one with relevant answer after it	Three questions generally distinct; answer relates to its question	One or two questions distinct; answer relates to its question	One or two questions generally distinct; answer unrelated to question	Questions not distinct; answer does not provide needed information	No distinct questions; no question-answer order
Voice	Shows writer's personal interest in all questions and in the answer	Generally shows writer's interest in questions and in the answer	Writer's interest in questions and in the answer clear at times	Some evidence of interest in the questions and answer	Little evidence of interest in the questions and answer	No evidence of involvement
Word Choice	*Who, what, when, where, why,* or *how*; many clear words; uses a pronoun	*Who, what, when, where, why,* or *how*; some clear words; uses a pronoun	Question words correct at times; no pronouns	Question words not always correct; words sometimes not clear	Question words used incorrectly	Vague or misused words
Sentences	Three interrogative sentences; an answer in declarative sentences	Three interrogative sentences; answer sentence(s) declarative	Two recognizable interrogative sentences; answer not very clear	One recognizable interrogative sentence; answer not very clear	One recognizable interrogative sentence	No recognizable interrogative sentence; sentences incorrect
Conventions	All questions end in question mark; few or no errors	Two or three questions end in clear question mark; no serious errors	Two questions end in clear question mark; few errors	One question ends in question mark; other errors	Question mark used correctly; few errors prevent understanding	Question marks not used correctly; errors prevent understanding

Rubric	5	4	3	2	1
Focus/Ideas	Three clear questions of interest to writer and a good answer to one	Three generally clear questions and a pertinent answer to one	Three questions; answer to one question unclear	Three questions but not all clear; attempts to answer one question	Rambling sentences, not formed as questions; no clear answer
Organization	Asks three questions distinctly, one with relevant answer after it	Three questions generally distinct; answer relates to its question	One or two questions generally distinct; answer unrelated to question	Questions not distinct; answer does not provide needed information	No distinct questions; no question-answer order
Voice	Shows writer's personal interest in all questions and in the answer	Generally shows writer's interest in questions and in the answer	Writer's interest in questions and in the answer clear at times	Little evidence of interest in the questions and answer	No evidence of involvement
Word Choice	*Who, what, when, where, why,* or *how*; many clear words; uses a pronoun	*Who, what, when, where, why,* or *how*; some clear words; uses a pronoun	Question words correct at times; no pronouns	Question words not always correct; words sometimes not clear	Vague or misused words
Sentences	Three interrogative sentences; an answer in declarative sentences	Three interrogative sentences; answer sentence(s) declarative	Two recognizable interrogative sentences; answer not very clear	One recognizable interrogative sentence; answer not very clear	No recognizable interrogative sentence; sentences incorrect
Conventions	All questions end in question mark; few or no errors	Two or three questions end in clear question mark; no serious errors	Two questions end in clear question mark; few serious errors	One question ends in question mark; other serious errors	Question marks not used correctly; errors prevent understanding

Rubric	4	3	2	1
Focus/Ideas	Three clear questions of interest to writer and a good answer to one	Three generally clear questions and a pertinent answer to one	Three questions but not all clear; attempts to answer one question	Rambling sentences, not formed as questions; no clear answer
Organization	Asks three questions distinctly, one with relevant answer after it	Three questions generally distinct; answer relates to its question	Questions not distinct; answer does not provide needed information	No distinct questions; no question-answer order
Voice	Shows writer's personal interest in all questions and in the answer	Generally shows writer's interest in questions and in the answer	Little evidence of interest in the questions and answer	No evidence of involvement
Word Choice	*Who, what, when, where, why,* or *how*; many clear words; uses a pronoun	*Who, what, when, where, why,* or *how*; some clear words	Question words not always correct; words sometimes not clear	Vague or misused words
Sentences	Three interrogative sentences; an answer in declarative sentences	Three interrogative sentences; answer sentence(s) declarative	Two recognizable interrogative sentences; answer not very clear	One or no recognizable interrogative sentence; sentences incorrect
Conventions	All questions end in question mark; few or no errors	Two or three questions end in clear question mark; no serious errors	One or two questions end in question mark; other serious errors	Question marks not used correctly; errors prevent understanding

Rubric	6	5	4	3	2	1
Focus/Ideas	Whole ad provides reasons for people to use the chosen machine	Ad provides some reasons for people to use the chosen machine	Ad provides unclear reasons for people to use the machine	Ad not always focused on reasons to use a chosen machine	Ad focused at times on reasons to use chosen machine	Ad not focused on reasons to use a machine
Organization	Machine identified early; vivid, descriptive reasons to use it	Machine identified early; clear reasons to use it	Machine identified early; unclear reasons to use it	Machine not identified early; weak reasons to use it	Machine identified late in ad; no reasons to use it	Machine not identified; no recognizable reasons to use it
Voice	Clearly aware of advertising purpose; informed and interested	Mostly aware of advertising purpose; interested	Writer's interest in machine unclear	Uncertain of advertising purpose; weak evidence of interest	Little evidence of interest or involvement	No evidence of involvement
Word Choice	Uses exact words to convince readers and pronouns for the machine	Some exact, persuasive words for purpose; one pronoun	Some exact, persuasive words attempted	Little attempt to use exact, persuasive words or pronouns	Persuasive words not attempted	Vague or misused words; no correct pronoun
Sentences	All sentences correctly constructed	Most sentences correctly constructed	Many sentences correctly constructed	Some sentences correctly constructed	Few sentences correctly constructed	Sentences incorrectly constructed
Conventions	Excellent control; correct use of all pronouns; few or no errors	Good control; correct use of pronoun or pronouns; no serious errors	Fair control; few incorrect pronouns; few serious errors	Limited control; some incorrect pronouns; errors hinder understanding	Weak control; incorrect pronouns; some errors hinder understanding	Many serious errors prevent understanding

Rubric	5	4	3	2	1
Focus/Ideas	Whole ad provides reasons for people to use the chosen machine	Ad provides some reasons for people to use the chosen machine	Ad provides unclear reasons for people to use the machine	Ad not always focused on reasons to use a chosen machine	Ad not focused on reasons to use a machine
Organization	Machine identified early; vivid, descriptive reasons to use it	Machine identified early; clear reasons to use it	Machine identified early; unclear reasons to use it	Machine not identified early; weak reasons to use it	Machine not identified; no recognizable reasons to use it
Voice	Clearly aware of advertising purpose; informed and interested	Mostly aware of advertising purpose; interested	Writer's interest in machine unclear	Uncertain of advertising purpose; weak evidence of interest	Little evidence of involvement
Word Choice	Uses exact words to convince readers and pronouns for the machine	Some exact, persuasive words for purpose; one pronoun	Some exact, persuasive words attempted	Little attempt to use exact, persuasive words or pronoun	Vague or misused words; no correct pronoun
Sentences	All sentences correctly constructed	Most sentences correctly constructed	Some sentences correctly constructed	Few sentences correctly constructed	Sentences incorrectly constructed
Conventions	Excellent control; correct use of all pronouns; few or no errors	Good control; correct use of pronoun or pronouns; no serious errors	Limited control; incorrect pronouns; few errors	Weak control; incorrect pronouns; errors hinder understanding	Many serious errors prevent understanding

Rubric	4	3	2	1
Focus/Ideas	Whole ad provides reasons for people to use the chosen machine	Ad provides some reasons for people to use the chosen machine	Ad not always focused on reasons to use a chosen machine	Ad not focused on reasons to use a machine
Organization	Machine identified early; vivid, descriptive reasons to use it	Machine identified early; clear reasons to use it	Machine not identified early; weak reasons to use it	Machine not identified; no recognizable reasons to use it
Voice	Clearly aware of advertising purpose; informed and interested	Mostly aware of advertising purpose; interested	Uncertain of advertising purpose; weak evidence of interest	Little evidence of involvement
Word Choice	Uses exact words to convince readers and pronouns for the machine	Some exact, persuasive words for purpose; one pronoun	Little attempt to use exact, persuasive words or pronoun	Vague or misused words; no correct pronoun
Sentences	All sentences correctly constructed	Most sentences correctly constructed	Few sentences correctly constructed	Sentences incorrectly constructed
Conventions	Excellent control; correct use of all pronouns; few or no errors	Good control; correct use of pronoun or pronouns; no serious errors	Weak control; incorrect pronouns; errors hinder understanding	Many serious errors prevent understanding

Rubric	6	5	4	3	2	1
Focus/Ideas	Excellent narrative from child's life, with real events about skills	Good narrative from child's life, mostly focused on events and skills	Fair narrative from child's life; generally focused on events	Narrative from child's life not clearly focused; events unclear	Little focus about events in child's narrative	No focus or details about events or skills in child's narrative
Organization	All sentences on topic, in time order from beginning to end	Most sentences on topic; generally in time order	Some sentences in time order	Some sentences not in time order; missing middle or end	Few sentences in time order	Events in no sensible time order
Voice	Writer's experiences and feelings clear and recognizable	Writer's experiences and feelings generally clear	Writer's experiences and feelings evident	Shows little of writer's experiences and feelings about events	Little sense of writer's experiences or feelings about events	Writer's feelings or experiences not evident
Word Choice	Vivid, exact words show how, when, and where; uses *I, me,* and *my*	Some vivid words telling how, when, and where; uses *I, me,* or *my*	Fair word choice, especially adverbs; occasionally misuses *I, me,* or *my*	Limited word choice, especially adverbs; misuses *I, me,* or *my*	Weak word choice; misuse or no use of *I, me,* or *my*	Vague or confusing word choice
Sentences	All sentences correct; sentences work together to tell writer's ideas	Most sentences correct; sentences tell writer's ideas	Few incorrect sentences; some sentences tell writer's ideas	Some incorrect sentences; some sentences tell writer's ideas	Many incorrect sentences; few sentences tell writer's ideas	Incomplete, incorrect, or unclear sentences; lacks coherence
Conventions	No mistakes or few mistakes, including use of *I, me,* and adverbs	No serious mistakes; correct use of *I, me,* and adverbs	Some mistakes; incorrect use of *I* or *me* and adverbs	Many mistakes; incorrect use of *I* or *me* and adverbs	Numerous mistakes; incorrect use of *I* or *me* and adverbs	Serious mistakes prevent understanding; misuse of *I* and *me*

Rubric	5	4	3	2	1
Focus/Ideas	Excellent narrative from child's life, with real events about skills	Good narrative from child's life, mostly focused on events and skills	Fair narrative from child's life; generally focused on events	Narrative from child's life not clearly focused; events unidentified	No focus or details about events or skills in child's narrative
Organization	All sentences on topic, in time order from beginning to end	Most sentences on topic; generally in time order	Some sentences in time order	Some sentences not in time order; missing middle or end	Events in no sensible time order
Voice	Writer's experiences and feelings clear and recognizable	Writer's experiences and feelings generally clear	Writer's experiences and feelings evident	Shows little of writer's experiences and feelings about events	Little sense of writer's experiences or feelings about events
Word Choice	Vivid, exact words show how, when, and where; uses *I, me,* and *my*	Some vivid words telling how, when, and where; uses *I, me,* or *my*	Fair word choice, especially adverbs; occasionally misuses *I, me,* or *my*	Limited word choice, especially adverbs; misuses *I, me,* or *my*	Vague or confusing word choice
Sentences	All sentences correct; sentences work together to tell writer's ideas	Most sentences correct; sentences tell writer's ideas	Few incorrect sentences; some sentences tell writer's ideas	Some incorrect sentences; some sentences tell writer's ideas	Incomplete, incorrect, or unclear sentences; lacks coherence
Conventions	No mistakes or few mistakes, including use of *I, me,* and adverbs	No serious mistakes; correct use of *I, me,* and adverbs	Some mistakes; incorrect use of *I* or *me* and adverbs	Numerous mistakes; incorrect use of *I* or *me* and adverbs	Serious mistakes prevent understanding; misuse of *I* and *me*

Rubric	4	3	2	1
Focus/Ideas	Excellent narrative from child's life, with real events about skills	Good narrative from child's life, mostly focused on events and skills	Narrative from child's life not clearly focused; events unidentified	No focus or details about events or skills in child's narrative
Organization	All sentences on topic, in time order from beginning to end	Most sentences on topic; generally in time order	Some sentences not in time order; missing middle or end	Events in no sensible time order
Voice	Writer's experiences and feelings clear and recognizable	Writer's experiences and feelings generally clear	Shows little of writer's experiences and feelings about events	Little sense of writer's experiences or feelings about events
Word Choice	Vivid, exact words show how, when, and where; uses *I, me,* and *my*	Some vivid words telling how, when, and where; uses *I, me,* or *my*	Limited word choice, especially adverbs; misuses *I, me,* or *my*	Vague or confusing word choice
Sentences	All sentences correct; sentences work together to tell writer's ideas	Most sentences correct; sentences tell writer's ideas	Some incorrect sentences; some sentences tell writer's ideas	Incomplete, incorrect, or unclear sentences; lacks coherence
Conventions	No mistakes or few mistakes, including use of *I, me,* and adverbs	No serious mistakes; correct use of *I, me,* and adverbs	Numerous mistakes; incorrect use of *I* or *me* and adverbs	Serious mistakes prevent understanding; misuse of *I* and *me*

POEM

Rubric	6	5	4	3	2	1
Focus/Ideas	Poem with strong focus on making an old thing new again	Poem focuses clearly on making an old thing new again	Poem generally focuses on making an old thing new again	Poem with weak focus on making an old thing new again	Resembles a poem; weak focus on topic	Rambling sentences or lines with unclear topic; not a poem
Organization	Carefully organized sentences; understandable actions or ideas	Organized sentences; generally tells understandable actions or ideas	Sentences generally organized; conveys some actions or ideas	Not consistently organized in lines	Rarely organized in lines	No recognizable arrangement
Voice	Imaginative and original, showing interest in topic and language	Mostly imaginative and original; some interest in topic and language	Tries to be original; little interest in topic	Tries to be imaginative; not original	Writer's imagination not present	Not imaginative or original
Word Choice	Vivid words, rhyming words, and two prepositional phrases	Many vivid words and rhyming words; one prepositional phrase	Some vivid words and rhyming words; one prepositional phrase	Few vivid words or rhyming words; attempt at prepositional phrase	Limited and dull word choice	Vague or incorrect words; no prepositional phrase
Sentences	Clear, correct sentences that sound good when read aloud	Mostly clear, correct sentences; sounds like a poem when read aloud	Few sentences unclear or correct; generally doesn't sound like a poem	Some sentences unclear or correct; doesn't sound like a poem	Most sentences unclear or correct	Incoherent or incorrect sentences
Conventions	Correct punctuation and prepositional phrases; few or no errors	Correct punctuation and prepositional phrases; no serious errors	Generally correct punctuation and prepositional phrase used; few serious errors	Some correct punctuation and prepositional phrases; some serious errors	Incorrect punctuation and prepositional phrases; serious errors	Many serious errors (including punctuation) prevent understanding

Rubric	5	4	3	2	1
Focus/Ideas	Poem with strong focus on making an old thing new again	Poem focuses clearly on making an old thing new again	Poem generally focuses on making an old thing new again	Poem with weak focus on making an old thing new again	Rambling sentences or lines with unclear topic; not a poem
Organization	Carefully organized sentences; understandable actions or ideas	Organized sentences; generally tells understandable actions or ideas	Sentences generally organized; conveys some actions or ideas	Not consistently organized in lines	No recognizable arrangement
Voice	Imaginative and original, showing interest in topic and language	Mostly imaginative and original; some interest in topic and language	Tries to be original; little interest in topic	Tries to be imaginative; not original	Not imaginative or original
Word Choice	Vivid words, rhyming words, and three prepositional phrases	Many vivid words and rhyming words; two prepositional phrases	Some vivid words and rhyming words; one prepositional phrase	Few vivid words or rhyming words; attempt at prepositional phrase	Vague or incorrect words; no prepositional phrase
Sentences	Clear, correct sentences that sound good when read aloud	Mostly clear, correct sentences; sounds like a poem when read aloud	Few sentences unclear or correct; doesn't sound like a poem	Most sentences unclear or incorrect; doesn't sound like a poem	Incoherent or incorrect sentences
Conventions	Correct punctuation and prepositional phrases; few or no errors	Correct punctuation and prepositional phrases; no serious errors	Occasionally incorrect punctuation and prepositional phrase used; serious errors	Incorrect punctuation and prepositional phrase; serious errors	Many serious errors (including punctuation) prevent understanding

Rubric	4	3	2	1
Focus/Ideas	Poem with strong focus on making an old thing new again	Poem focuses clearly on making an old thing new again	Poem with weak focus on making an old thing new again	Rambling sentences or lines with unclear topic; not a poem
Organization	Carefully organized sentences; understandable actions or ideas	Organized sentences; generally tells understandable actions or ideas	Not consistently organized in lines; conveys some actions or ideas	No recognizable arrangement
Voice	Imaginative and original, showing interest in topic and language	Mostly imaginative and original; some interest in topic and language	Tries to be imaginative; not original	Not imaginative or original
Word Choice	Vivid words, rhyming words, and two prepositional phrases	Some vivid words and rhyming words; one prepositional phrase	Few vivid words or rhyming words; attempt at prepositional phrase	Vague or incorrect words; no prepositional phrase
Sentences	Clear, correct sentences that sound good when read aloud	Mostly clear, correct sentences; sounds like a poem when read aloud	Most sentences unclear or incorrect; doesn't sound like a poem	Incoherent or incorrect sentences
Conventions	Correct punctuation and prepositional phrases; few or no errors	Correct punctuation and prepositional phrases; no serious errors	Incorrect punctuation and prepositional phrase; serious errors	Many serious errors (including punctuation) prevent understanding

1   Kreis / Stern / Circle / Star, 2015
Garn, Nägel / thread, nails, 700 cm (Länge / length)

2   Luckhardt 3, 2009
Glas, Silikon / glass, silicone, 30 x 108 x 80 cm

3   Der Blick in die Zukunft / Future Prospect, 2015
Garn, Nägel, Blei / thread, nails, lead, 100 x 180 x 70 cm (Vitrine / showcase),
325 cm (Länge der Fadenverspannung / length of thread-work)

4.1 Nr. 369 / No. 369, 2015
4.2 Nr. 370 / No. 370, 2015
4.3 Nr. 371 / No. 371, 2015
4.4 Nr. 372 / No. 372, 2015
4.5 Nr. 373 / No. 373, 2015
>>> Gouache auf Papier / gouache on paper, je / each 24 x 17 cm

5   Moderne Zeiten / Modern Times, 2015
glasierte Keramik, Papier, Tabak / glazed ceramics, paper, tobacco,
100 x 180 x 70 cm (Vitrine / showcase)

6   27 Fotos / 27 photos, 7,5 x 200 cm (gesamt / total)

7.1 Lorenz Attractor, 2015
7.2 Paradoxon / Fibonacci / Paradox / Fibonacci, 2015
7.3 Schwarzes Loch / Weißes Loch / Black Hole / White Hole, 2015
>>> Stoff, Perlen, Garn / fabric, beads, thread,
jeweils zweiteilig / each in two parts, 300 x 280 cm

8.1 Kallmorgen (Spiegel-Hochhaus) / Kallmorgen (Spiegel Tower), 2015
armierter Beton / reinforced concrete, 76,5 x 122 x 63 cm

8.2 Kallmorgen (Spiegel-Pavillon) / Kallmorgen (Spiegel Pavilion), 2015
armierter Beton / reinforced concrete, 25,5 x 64 x 44 cm

8.3 Kallmorgen (IBM-Hochhaus) / Kallmorgen (IBM Tower), 2015
Spiegelglas, Pappe / mirror glass, cardboard, 4 x 310 x 285 cm

8.4 Schneeberg / Pile of Snow, 2015
glasierte Keramik / glazed ceramics, 16 x 56 x 24,5 cm

9   Kallmorgen (Kaispeicher A), 2015
armierter Beton / reinforced concrete, 70,5 x 120,5 x 78 cm

10.1 Ascher (Elbphilharmonie, Dach) / Ashtray (Elbphilharmonie, Roof), 2015
glasierte Keramik / glazed ceramics, 10,5 x 45 x 22 cm

10.2 Ascher (Spiegel-Hochhaus) / Ashtray (Spiegel Tower), 2015
glasierte Keramik / glazed ceramics, 30 x 32,5 x 12,5 cm

10.3 Ascher (Ernst Barlach Haus) / Ashtray (Ernst Barlach Haus), 2015
glasierte Keramik / glazed ceramics, 19,5 x 32 x 20 cm

11.1 Ernst Barlach: „Nöck", 1903 / 04
glasiertes Steinzeug / glazed stoneware, 15,4 x 13 x 13,7 cm

11.2 Ernst Barlach: „Triton" / "Merman", 1903 / 04
glasiertes Steinzeug / glazed stoneware, 8,5 x 25,2 x 16,2 cm
>>> Ernst Barlach Haus Hamburg

12   Zeitmaschinen / Time Machines, zweite Hälfte 20. Jahrhundert / 2nd half of the
20th century, Papier, Metall, Kunststoff / paper, metal, plastic,
207 x 130 x 55 cm (Vitrine / showcase)

13   Postmoderne Ruine / Post-modern Ruin, 2013
faserarmierter Beton, Porzellan / reinforced concrete, porcelain, 92 x 49 x 49 cm

courtesy Esther Schipper, Berlin, Galerie Jocelyn Wolff, Paris, und / and Galerie nächst
St. Stephan Rosemarie Schwarzwälder, Wien / Vienna

Dieses Buch erscheint anlässlich der Ausstellung
This book is published in conjunction with the exhibition

ISA MELSHEIMER
Kontrastbedürfnis / Need for Contrast

Ernst Barlach Haus — Stiftung Hermann F. Reemtsma, Hamburg
12. Juli — 4. Oktober 2015 / 12 July — 4 October, 2015

Konzept / Concept: Isa Melsheimer und / and Karsten Müller; Herausgeber / Editor:
Karsten Müller; Übersetzung / Translation: Michael Turnbull; Fotos / Photo credits:
Andreas Weiss; Gestaltung / Graphic design: Susanne Bax; Lithografie / Lithography:
Frische Grafik; Herstellung / Production: DZA Druckerei zu Altenburg GmbH

E R N S T   B A R L A C H   H A U S

Ernst Barlach Haus — Stiftung Hermann F. Reemtsma
Jenischpark, Baron-Voght-Straße 50a, 22609 Hamburg, Germany
Tel. +49 (0)40 — 82 60 85, Fax +49 (0)40 — 82 64 15
info@barlach-haus.de, www.barlach-haus.de

VERLAG FÜR MODERNE KUNST

VfmK Verlag für moderne Kunst GmbH
Salmgasse 4a, 1030 Wien / Vienna, Austria
Tel. +43 (0)680 — 140 57 39
hello@vfmk.org, www.vfmk.org

Die Deutsche Nationalbibliothek verzeichnet diese Publikation in der Deutschen
Nationalbibliografie; detaillierte bibliografische Daten sind im Internet über
http://dnb.ddb.de abrufbar. / Die Deutsche Nationalbibliothek lists this publication
in the Deutsche Nationalbibliografie; detailed bibliographic data is available in
the Internet at http://dnb.ddb.de.

Vertrieb / Distribution: D, A und Europa / D, A and Europe: LKG, www.lkg-va.de;
CH: AVA, www.ava.ch; UK: Cornerhouse Publications, www.cornerhouse.org;
USA: D.A.P., www.artbook.com